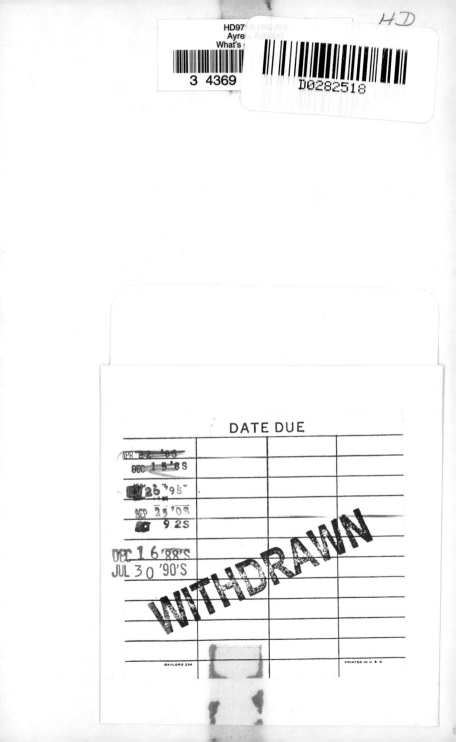

What's Good for GM . . .

What's Good for GM . . .

BY

EDWARD AYRES

AURORA PUBLISHERS INCORPORATED
NASHVILLE/LONDON

CONTENTS

Acknowledgments

I would like to thank Herb Hamburger for sharing some of his trenchant perceptions of the relationship between humanity and technology; Bill Lohr for his contagious anger about the insensitivities of the institutions which dominate our lives; Sue Simon for her help in digging up obscure and usually outrageous information; Bernie Trilling for helping to create order out of the chaos of my manuscript; my employer Ted Taylor, for making it possible to write this book and earn a living at the same time; and my wife Bonnie, for her constant assurances that GM has no more right to monopolize my life—book or no book—than it has to monopolize the American automobile industry.

Special thanks are due to Ray Watts, counsel for the Monopoly Subcommittee of the Senate Small Business Committee, who supplied valuable material and made a number of important corrections in the final draft; and most of all to my brother Bob, who made available to me the benefits of his years of experience in the fields of transportation technology and technological forecasting, and whose idea it was to do this book in the first place.

Foreword

The paradoxes of the American brand of free enterprise, with all its unparalleled comforts, mobility and staggering problems are nowhere more visible than in the role of the automobile and its impact on the modern life style.

The automobile gave Americans mobility and independence. It made it possible to move comfortably and efficiently beyond the cities and develop the suburban countryside, to quickly reach centers for employment and recreation areas.

Edward Ayres graphically describes the American four-wheeled society in this book when he writes: "In the United States, almost anything a person can do can be—and often is—done in a car. People eat, listen to music, watch movies, make love, sleep, cash checks, mail letters and have babies in cars. They go hunting in cars, hike—so to speak—through the woods in cars, and end their lives in cars."

Anything that became so integral a part of American life also became a vital part of the economy. Some 14 million members of the American work force, about 16 percent, are employed in the manufacture, distribution, maintenance and commercial use of motor vehicles. It is estimated that, economically, the automobile accounts for 13 percent of the now more than $900 billion Gross National Product, or about $117 billion annually.

1

But all that couldn't and didn't continue without a disastrous reaction. The demands for the automobile in a consumer-oriented society meant demands for more roads, streets and highways that would carry motorists more rapidly from place to place and more paved areas to park the resting autos that had arrived or were waiting to go someplace else.

Transportation dependence on the automobile became almost total, and this country became enmeshed in a cycle of building more roads because more people were buying cars; then more cars were built and sold because the roads were there and other ways of traveling on the ground were not.

With it all came the mounting accidental deaths, unchecked resource consumption, junk disposal, air pollution, noise, traffic jams, human dislocations and disruptions, destruction of city neighborhoods, uglification of both the urban and rural scene, and the nearly total collapse of mass transit systems.

We can never know what this country would have been like if we had decided in the mid-fifties, not just to build more roads, but to spend a like amount of money for other systems of transportation. Although we can never know, it is a safe assumption that what "might have been" would be significantly better than what is.

The first indication of the disparity in values is the amount of federal funds spent on the Interstates since 1956 and the amount spent in support of both urban and interurban rapid rail transportation systems since 1965: The Interstates, $32 billion. Rail transit, well under $1 billion.

The next interesting comparison is that the American Transit Association estimates the country needs to spend $28.2 billion for mass transit in the next ten years, while the American Association of State Highway Officials projects a need for $320 billion for highways over the next fifteen years, or $20 billion a year for planning, construction and maintenance.

In this book, Ayres points out the great impact the auto industry has had and the special influence it has throughout all levels of government. It raises questions that were also raised at hearings of two subcommittees of the Senate Select Committee on Small Business that I conducted jointly with Senator Wayne Morse. He asks, for example, why an industry which claims to be highly competitive is failing to produce many of the consumer benefits expected of a healthy market and why the automotive industry lacks the social responsibility to take the leadership in environmental protection.

Ayres offers a welcome challenge to the notion that growth, measured in units of automotive production, is a value to which all others must be subordinated. In the rush of hurrying off to work each day, he argues, "the fact that some of the things which have suffered as a result of this compulsive push for more and more production might contribute as much to the national well-being as things being produced, has been largely overlooked."

Much of the book is concerned with the frustrations of the car owner burdened with costs he can't keep down. Ayres is sympathetic with the problems of the auto dealer. He suggests possible future alliances between car dealers and car buyers to combat the auto makers' clever exploitation of both groups.

His emphasis, however, is on the social costs the automobile has imposed on society, driver and non-driver, in air pollution, congestion, noise, accidental deaths and mutilations.

Ayres feels that the institution of the American automobile is not a total evil, but instead a good of major importance that has been unnecessarily abused by its producers and consumers alike.

This compact book is a valuable source of information on the confusing success-failure role the automobile has played in American free enterprise. Ayres believes, however, that the automobile, freed of its deadly pollutants and part of a balanced mass ground transportation system, can continue to benefit the progress and mobility of this society.

Sen. Gaylord Nelson

Introduction
THE MOCK OF EXCELLENCE

One characteristic of a capitalist society is that its industries, like its people, sometimes acquire public images by which they are quickly transformed into heroes or villains. The space industry endeared itself to 100 million TV viewers with the success of the Apollo moonshot, while the oil industry has provoked widespread bitterness with its depletion allowances and leaking ships; but the industry which best knows the whims of public approval or disapproval is the automobile manufacturing industry. For fifty of its first sixty years it was the hero, making vast contributions to the culture, economy, and national security of the United States. These contributions are well known to most Americans, partly because the industry's public relations men have done their jobs extraordinarily well, and partly because the automobile is one product of our civilization by which no one remains unaffected.

In the last decade, the auto industry has turned from hero to villain, not only because of the changing reputation of American cars, but also because of growing apprehensions about the enormous companies which manufacture them. Of course, the contributions of the industry—the assembly line, the "unification" of rural and urban America, the emergency production of arms in World War II— have not been forgotten; the Automobile Manufacturers Association speaks of these achievements with an uncritical pride that has not flagged in the years that have passed since they occurred. However, the public knows now that these are things of the past. The present has brought desperate complications to what was once a fairly simple transaction between the maker of a car and the driver to whom it was sold. The makers, accustomed to praise, are now being overwhelmed by criticism—not only from consumers but from dealers, insurance companies, suppliers, economists, ecologists, engineers, and—increasingly— politicians.

In some eyes, the auto industry of the past ten years has seemed a brutish Goliath confronted by righteous Davids. To others, it has seemed more like an innocent Gulliver being poked at by merciless Lilliputians. Certainly, there are opportunists among those who have joined the movement to "control" the burgeoning influence of the auto makers. It is equally certain that critics have ganged up on Detroit for good reasons, and that whatever may be said in praise of cars, the glory which once was theirs has been badly tarnished. The era of the untamed automobile appears likely to come to a rapid close in the 1970s, but just how the conflict between Detroit and its various antagonists will be resolved depends on the resolution of four critical issues.

First, there is the question of economy. There can be no denying that the automobile manufacturing industry consumes impressive quantities of steel, oil, rubber, and glass; employs hundreds of thousands of workers; pays billions of dollars in taxes; and serves as the dominant element of a network of more than 800,000 automotive businesses accounting for some 13 percent of the Gross National Product of the United States.[1] Obviously, this industry is one of the great strengths of the American economy.

What is not so visible to the casual observer is that the auto industry strengthens one part of the economy only at the expense of others. When big businesses flex their financial muscles, small businesses are squeezed and sometimes crushed. General Motors, Ford, and Chrysler pour riches into the coffers of government, the campaign chests of influential legislators, and the charities of Gary and Detroit. Madison Avenue and Capitol Hill praise the makers for their good citizenship, ignoring the fact that hundreds of small businesses are being destroyed by the very process which enables the auto industry to claim credit for keeping the economy strong. The manufacturers call this process "competition," but economists know better. The auto manufacturing industry is actually a highly concentrated oligopoly, and the effects of oligopoly, on the business community and on the consumer, are devastating. What appears to be competition is largely promotion. What is sometimes called "supply-and-demand" is largely a hollow slogan of the manufacturers, who supply new cars to the nation's dealers with little regard for the demands of the public, except insofar as these demands are originally shaped by the manufacturers. Imperiled small businessmen, ranging from independent radio producers to retail auto dealers, along with millions of customers who have begun to realize that the quality of the American car has grown worse instead of better, have given notice to the country that they are determined to resist the giant manufacturers' growing infringements on their economic rights.

Second, there is the issue of the cities. It is hard to imagine what American cities, particularly the sprawling newer ones such as Dallas and Los Angeles, would do without cars. At the same time, it is horrible to imagine what they *will* do if the stranglehold of cars continues much longer. The automobile and its makers have contributed heavily to the decay of the American city. Central business districts which were once thriving centers of commercial and cultural activity are being needlessly choked to death. Congested streets have the same effect on cities as congested arteries have on the human organism: they constrict vital circulation, interfering with the city's most essential functions. The view that circulation can be improved by adding more arteries has been carefully nurtured

by the highway and auto interests, but case after
case has shown the contrary to be true: more roads
simply draw more cars into the cities, which have
already yielded half of their space to private transportation. Cities are ill-suited to accommodate both
people and cars, particularly the kinds of cars produced by Detroit. With Frankensteinian irony, it
is the people who have been forced to yield to the
cars by which they are supposed to be served. Yet
different policies, both in the designing of cars and
in the roles cars play in urban transportation, could
have relieved much of the congestion, cleaned the
air, and brought new vitality into the cities years
ago. Such policies have been steadfastly resisted
by the automobile manufacturing industry.

The third issue is public responsibility. The auto
industry in its present form has a disproportionate
influence in the affairs of state. Even when they
are acting individually, the great manufacturing
companies can wield enormous clout in the federal
government, as can the giants in a small number
of other industries. The auto companies do not,
as a rule, operate individually when it comes to
exerting influence. Their interests are identical and
mutual, and the obstacle they pose to opponents
of these interests is formidable. The "Big Three"
have more wealth, and in some ways more power,
than any state in the union and more than most
countries. Industry policies are generally set by
General Motors and followed, with only minor deviations, by the other auto manufacturing compa-

nies, but while these companies loom as big as governments in the lives of the public, they are—unlike any reasonably democratic government—unresponsive to public approval or disapproval of their policies. In theory, the competitive structure of the market should serve as a means of public control. In the oligopoly of the auto industry, however, competition has shifted to the retail level, leaving the manufacturers free to pursue their interests unchecked. Worse, there is no meaningful communication between the industry and the public, to whom the manufacturers seem to have few obligations. Refusals of the manufacturers to talk about their public policies constitute, in the case of such an influential industry, as much of a threat to the public's "right to know" as would a severe curtailing of freedom of the press.

The fourth issue is that of life on earth. In the past quarter century, over a million Americans have died in automobile collisions, some as a result of either their own carelessness or that of other drivers, and some as a result of the institutionalized carelessness of the auto industry. Manufacturers' policies in the past twenty-five years have consistently subordinated the well-being of consumers to the well-being of the manufacturers, and the pressures of the 1960s have not substantially changed these policies. While motorists continue to die in record numbers, the pollution caused by automobile exhaust imperils life on earth—not only human life, but forests and crops and every form of wildlife

as well—on an even greater scale. Cars have become
instruments of destruction more potent than war,
not only because they fail to protect their occupants in thousands of collisions every day, but
because they pump more poison into people's lungs
than all the factories, powerplants, and refineries
in America. Yet neither the frailty of its structure
nor the toxicity of its exhaust is inherent in the
nature of a car; both could have been remedied
long ago if the manufacturers had spent money
they could easily have afforded to spend. The
manufacturers resisted such expense and continue
to do so, despite well-contrived appearances to the
contrary. Meanwhile, more Americans are killed
by cars in one year than by war, drugs, and crime
put together, and the number killed or weakened
by automotive pollution has never even been measured.

More broadly, there is the issue of "life" in the
sense of "quality of existence." If there is any truth
in the idea that "we are what we eat," then it is
equally true that "we are what we do." In the
United States, almost anything a person can do
can be, and often is, done in a car. People eat, listen
to music, watch movies, make love, sleep, cash
checks, mail letters, and have babies in cars. They
go hunting in cars, hike, so to speak, through the
woods in cars, and end their lives in cars. Many
of these activities have become so inextricably car-
oriented that the original institutions themselves
have changed. Drive-in restaurants, drive-in mov-

ies, drive-in banks, and even drive-in funeral parlors are built to accommodate those who cannot (or would rather not) climb out of their cars except when absolutely necessary. Even the traditional rugged American "outdoor types," the hunters, fishermen, hikers, and campers, have been seduced by cars. Sales of four-wheel "recreational" vehicles boomed in the late 1960s, indicating that even people who love the outdoors are growing to like the idea of rolling through the wilderness on wheels. In all this automania there lurks the danger of a slowly diminishing quality of existence, of a fading appreciation of the experiences cars have usurped from the bodies and senses of men. With cities already lying in a state of near-exhaustion from the usurpations *they* have suffered (both automotive and otherwise), this danger may be more insidious than those of either accident or disease.

None of these issues have as yet been resolved. How they will be resolved in the 1970s will be of acute interest, not only to the makers of cars but to anyone who is affected by the manufacture or consumption of automobiles. The impact of any major changes precipitated by these issues, whether in the structure of the industry or the nature of the car, will be felt by tens of millions of Americans at the manufacturing and marketing levels alone. Coming changes in propulsion technology, for example—not the superficial style changes ballyhooed by the industry each year, but real changes in the nature of the vehicle—will cause tremors throughout the entire economy. Powerful lobbies are lined up to prevent such changes, but the forces they oppose may well be unstoppable.

At the level of consumption, the impact of change is likely to be even more widespread. Few activities demand more attention, time, energy, or money than the ownership of a car. Automobiles account for 16 percent of all primary energy consumed in the United States.[2] In 1968, Americans traveled one trillion (1,000,000,000,000) miles by car.[3] The car is primarily a short-distance mode of transportation (60 percent of all automobile trips are five miles or less); yet, in spite of competition from planes, trains, and buses, 86 percent of all travelers making *long* trips in 1968—including 97 percent of those traveling in groups of five or more—went by car.[4] That one mode should so dominate the movement of people when at least a dozen other modes are available [5] is in itself intriguing; but when the domestic production and distribution of this dominant mode is controlled by just four manufacturing corporations, and the marketing behavior of those corporations is in turn controlled largely by *one* corporation,[6] the resulting concentration of power, not merely economic power, but political and social and cultural power, takes on alarming proportions. Clearly, the influence of the auto industry on *activity in general* is enormous, and for that reason alone, it deserves the careful scrutiny of those who share responsibility for the public welfare. Aside from the murderous effects of accidents and pollution, there is great disparity between the frantic attention given to the influence of such products of our civilization as drugs and TV, and that given to the impact of cars, on the bodies and minds of their users. What this impact has come to be and how it is affected by the concentration of power in the auto industry is the subject of this book. It is a question that concerns not only a measurable toll taken by the industry in lives, property, and environmental resources, but something immeasurably deeper. At root, it is a question of what becomes of an individual's control of his own destiny in a nation where destinies are plotted increasingly in the isolated board rooms of giant corporations, whose interests and operations are far-removed from the arena of ordinary human activity.

I—MOVERS

On an October afternoon in 1969, twelve University of Minnesota students marched into downtown Minneapolis dragging a wooden cart. Passersby paid little attention, although the ceremony the students were about to perform signified the rising of a new passion in America and the beginning of a movement which, in the next few months, was to bring unprecedented challenges to the traditional roles of giant manufacturing corporations, ponderous federal regulatory agencies, and certain other "sacred cows" of the world's most productive economy.

In the bottom of the cart lay the motor of a dead car. Such motors are not an uncommon sight, since over six million are discarded each year, but this one was making its last ride in a unique manner. The students, having joined a swelling army of Americans concerned about the impact of the conventional (internal combustion) automobile engine on the quality of the air, had decided to express their impatience in the most graphic way possible. As a small crowd gathered, the students dropped the motor into a grave, covered it with dirt, and solemnly declared an end to the tyranny of the internal combustion engine over the lungs, lives and wallets of the American people.

In reality, of course, the era of the internal combustion engine was not over at all. Even as a young minister read a quiet eulogy over the hated object—" . . . Ashes to Ashes, Dust to Dust; For the Sake of Mankind, Iron to Rust"—cars powered by internal combustion engines roared past, pumping their exhaust into the air. The conventional automobile engine is the largest single polluter of air in the world, but in October 1969, not a single manufacturer of American cars was selling anything else.

The significance of the funeral was not that it marked a change in manufacturers' policies, but that it was the acting-out of a powerful wish by a group of consumers. Like the fantasy story of Hansel and Gretel, in which children convert evil to good by turning a witch into gingerbread, the funeral was an expression not only of impatience, but of the helplessness of the consumer, who has no control over that which he must consume, and can take only symbolic actions against the causes of his frustration.

The symbolism of the great Minnesota Engine Burial did not go unnoticed. The ceremony was filmed by NBC and later appeared on a network show. To some viewers, it vindicated long-accumulated frustrations. The worst effects of air pollution are not always visible, but one can't help noticing such things as the thick black film that coats the windshield of a car left on a city street for several days. Yet one never knows where the coating came from, what dangers it represents, or who to blame for it. Nearly everyone had heard talk that the world could become unfit for habitation before the end of the century.[7] Such talk was not new to Americans, who were growing more and more used to the idea of always being under the shadow of omnipotent evil. There had been the Bomb, and there had been Communism, and now there was Pollution. The need to strike back at something tangible was growing stronger. Here, in a piece of palpable machinery, was a specific culprit, and the satisfaction of watching it buried was exquisite.[8]

To other viewers, particularly those in the more affluent suburbs of Detroit, the ritual verged on blasphemy. America takes its manufactured products—its computers and electric razors and color TVs—seriously, but if there was ever a piece of machinery with the status of a god, it is the engine which powers the American car.[9] Generations of high school boys have listened in awe to the growl it makes when it explodes its fuel, while their fathers have spoken reverently of its role in the American economy. Nearly two decades after the discovery that the internal combustion engine was a threat to the well-being of millions of Americans, faith in the ancient machine remained largely unshaken. In 1969, *Time* stated "the U.S. economy is geared directly to the mighty internal combustion engine" and that "conversion of the nation's 101 million vehicles to electricity, even if possible, would cause nothing less than an economic trauma." The magazine claimed to be paraphrasing a well-known economist, Bruce C. Netschert, who had just delivered a paper on the subject. Privately, however, Netschert claimed he had said no such thing.[10] Apparently, the main significance of the *Time* comment was that it reflected a widespread prejudice. Throughout the 1960s, it was almost universally believed that to pull the internal combustion engine out of the American car would be to pull the cornerstone out of the American economy. The manufacturers nurtured this belief carefully, mobilizing enormous lobbying efforts to dramatize the unfeasibility of any alternatives to the smoky little power plant which had been their baby for so long.

Because little was known about the chemistry of air pollution until the 1960s, few people connected pollution with cars. The earliest concern was more with filth than with poison, and filthy air appeared to come primarily from factories, power plants, and refineries.[11] Whereas a car leaves only a faint bluish plume of exhaust in its wake (the main ingredient is invisible carbon monoxide), a smokestack belches large gouts of dark smoke. Measurements have established, however, that cars pump ninety million tons of waste into the air each year, compared to only thirty million from manufacturing, fifteen million from power plants, eight million from heating, and three million from waste disposal.[12] In his book *The Breath of Life,* chemist Donald E. Carr concludes that "of all sources of hazardous air pollution, the automobile in urban centers is so overwhelmingly the cause of trouble that one can, in noncoal-burning communities, regard it essentially as the only source."[13] (Carr spent a lifetime doing chemical research on automotive fuels and was still working as a semiretired consultant to Phillips Petroleum when he decided to unburden himself of what he had learned about the ecological impacts of automobile exhaust. Immediately after his book was published, Phillips Petroleum received an angry telephone call from General Motors—and Carr was fired on the spot.)

For five decades, nobody had questioned the "right" of a car to dump its fumes into the air people breathe. There is no essential difference between a car spitting effluents into a city's air supply and a cow defecating in the spring from which a camper dips his drinking water. The public, however, was unaccustomed to thinking of air in such terms, perhaps because it is still easier to think of air as empty space rather than as a commodity which can be damaged, or even used up. For the first twenty years after the end of World War II, Americans were far more preoccupied with production levels and profit margins than with the long-range effects of production on the environment. It was not until the physiological, economic, and aesthetic implications of automobile pollution were made explicit that the pedestal of the internal combustion engine began to tremble for the first time in half a century.

The peculiar chemistry by which automobile exhaust combines with fresh air to create a thick, hazardous pall over such cities as Los Angeles and New York was first discovered in 1953 by Dr. Arlie Haagen-Smit of the California Institute of Technology, a Dutchman who soon came to be known as "Dr. Smog." (In 1969, Haagen-Smit was made chairman of President Nixon's new Task Force on Air Pollution.) In the decade which followed the initial discovery, study after study demonstrated that air pollution is an important factor in the occurrence and worsening of chronic diseases, as well as a major contributor to widespread economic losses.[14]

Carbon monoxide, nearly all of which comes from motor vehicles, was found to be associated with headache, insomnia, fatigue, shortness of breath, muscular twitching, drowsiness, unsteady gait, cramps, coughing, vomiting, perversion of taste and smell, loss of feeling in the forearms, abnormal brain waves, speech defects, and other maladies.[15] In heavy doses, of course, carbon monoxide is deadly. As Carr puts it, "One of the striking things about CO is the dreadful simplicity with which it kills." Because carbon monoxide has an affinity for hemoglobin 210 times as strong as that of oxygen, it quickly replaces the oxygen in the blood of anyone breathing it. Russian hygienists have recommended that the maximum concentration of CO allowable for safe breathing be set at one part per million parts of air;[16] yet the concentration of this gas in the air surrounding heavy traffic, such as that which is generated during rush hours in many American cities, occasionally reaches a level of 100 parts per million.[17] In the raw exhaust, the concentration is about 35,000 parts per million—enough, as many suicides have verified, to cause a rapid and relatively painless extinction of life.[18]

There is also evidence that many auto accidents which are blamed on drunken driving are actually the result of carbon monoxide poisoning. Some of the symptoms of such poisoning are the same as those of alcoholic intoxication. Few highway police are likely to think twice when a driver staggers as he gets out of his automobile, or when his eyes fail to "track." "We will never know," says Carr, "how many fatal accidents have been caused by preliminary CO-dopiness of drivers to the point of helplessness or even coma, since there has been no attempt to determine by autopsy the incidence of carboxylhemoglobin in the blood of the victims." The first symptom of such drowsiness is likely to be a sudden tightening across the forehead, something most drivers attribute to boredom or fatigue. Cars are supposed to be built well enough to keep carbon monoxide out of the passenger compartment, but leaks are alarmingly common. In 1969, General Motors recalled 2,570,914 Chevrolets because of the possibility that faulty exhaust systems would allow fumes to enter the interior of the car.[19]

Two other ingredients of automobile exhaust, hydrocarbons and oxides of nitrogen, are just as deadly as carbon monoxide and even more insidious. Some hydrocarbons attack the membranes of eyes and lungs, causing millions of city dwellers to complain of eye irritations and respiratory difficulties. Those which don't attack people attack plants, often with devastating results. A hydrocarbon called ethylene causes spinach to wither and orchids to die. Orchid growers, previously driven out of Southern California by the proliferation of cars, are now being similarly threatened in San Francisco.[20]

Together with oxides of nitrogen, hydrocarbons react with atmospheric ozone to produce photochemical "smog," a bottle-brown substance once thought to be a simple mixture of smoke and fog. The reaction which produces smog is not fully understood, but it is known that its main ingredients come from the tailpipes and crankcases of millions of cars. It is also known that smog has a dangerous capacity for weakening the human organism, making it more vulnerable to diseases of the lungs and heart, and occasionally destroying it in sudden sweeps of affliction reminiscent of plague. A California health survey in 1956 showed that 74 percent of the people in Los Angeles were affected by smog.[21] Since then the problem has worsened and spread, despite the use of antismog devices on cars. In 1968, doctors in Los Angeles urged more than ten thousand people to leave the city because of air pollution's harmful effects on them.[22] In 1969, a report from the American Public

Health Association's annual conference claimed that "badly polluted air frequently causes ten to twenty deaths a day in New York City." In the same city, nylons gradually dissolve in smog, and the facades of buildings crumble prematurely.[23] Along the Eastern coast, smog damage to vegetable crops amounts to $18 million a year.[24] Studies in both the U.S. and abroad suggest a possible connection between air pollution and lung cancer.[25] In the Philadelphia Zoo (which is bordered by the heavily trafficked Schuylkill Expressway) the incidence of fatal cancer in birds and animals has risen 600 percent since 1905, the beginning of the automotive era. It would be hard to blame this increase on cigarettes. In the brief span since 1960, a span during which automotive sales mushroomed and the country became increasingly enamored of high-compression engines, the death rate from emphysema increased nearly tenfold. By 1968, the news was getting around that emphysema (a hardening of lung membranes which has been linked directly with air pollution) had become the fastest growing cause of death (among humans) in America.[26]

Naturally, the main effect of this news in the 1960s was to stimulate new legislation. The Clean Air Act, passed in December 1963, allowed state and local governments to assume responsibility for controlling the pollution of their own air spaces. However, while local programs sometimes succeeded in regulating stationary sources of pollution, they were not easily applied to cars, which moved from place to place. The act was therefore amended in 1965 to provide national standards for motor vehicle emissions, beginning in 1968. It was soon apparent that the auto manufacturers could not— or would not—be easily persuaded to meet the projected standards simply by modifying the internal combustion engine.

After Haagen-Smit's discovery, fifteen years passed during which Detroit made virtually no effort to reduce pollution by installing control devices on cars. The makers disliked the control devices, not only because they interfered with performance ("it's like making a car wear a condom," said one), but also because they did not think such contraptions would be profitable. Not one company volunteered to install such devices until required by law to do so.

Once the control devices were assured by Congress, however, the auto makers shifted tactics abruptly. Before, they had laughed at the pollution issue and had brazenly tried to avoid compromising their engine designs in any way. Now, with Congress showing a surprising new capacity to stand up to the auto lobby, it was clear that the pollution issue would have to be taken somewhat more seriously. Almost overnight, the manufacturers changed their stance on control devices from strenuous opposition to enthusiastic support. Their opposition, of course, had been carefully shielded from the public. Their support was now widely advertised. Much of the public was led to believe that the auto companies were installing control devices because of a sense of public responsibility.

In addition to deceiving nearly everyone but the government, the industry's show of support for control devices served an even more devious purpose. Faced with a choice between cleaning up its old engine or building a new one, Detroit suddenly became very optimistic about cleaning up the old one. In the days before the emissions law, the makers had expressed great doubts about the efficacy of such devices. The technological difficulties were enormous, they had said. Now, suddenly, all the difficulties had evaporated!

On May 26, 1969, readers of *Automotive News,* the industry's weekly newspaper, must have blinked twice at a headline reading SMOG BATTLE WON, INDUSTRY SAYS. The story claimed that GM president Edward Cole, Ford vice chairman Arjay Miller, and Chrysler president Virgil Boyd all "strongly supported" a statement by Chrysler engineer Charles M. Heinen, that "when all cars are equipped with the controls that the 1970 California cars are equipped with, then we will have won the battle."[27]

Heinen's statement drew a swift reaction. "It will come as quite a shock to those on the receiving end of air pollution to learn that the battle is won," said Los Angeles Pollution Control official Robert Barsky.[28] Barsky then listed several problems which Heinen had somehow overlooked.

Like any good engineer, Heinen had supported his assertion with figures. Unfortunately, his figures had little to do with the amount of pollution in the atmosphere in May 1969. They had nothing to do with the amount of pollution which would have to be removed from the atmosphere to abate the destruction of property and life. They had to do only with the likelihood that pollution from cars would soon decline—slightly—to a level of concentration which Heinen had apparently decided was all right for Americans to breathe. The fact that that level was purely arbitrary, and far above the levels which some medical authorities consider safe, had apparently not entered Heinen's thinking.

In any case, Heinen's figures did not mean what they purported to mean. They had been based on tests of specially tuned models, not on automobiles as they roll off the production line. There is, as anyone who is familiar with the internal combustion engine can attest, a considerable difference. Furthermore, the testing method used was inapplicable to mass inspections, and mass inspections are essential if pollution control is to be assured with engines which are not inherently nonpolluting. Even GM chairman James Roche, the biggest wheel in the whole automotive business, could have told Heinen that. As Roche ruefully acknowledged in 1969, "We have to use computers, exhaust chambers, and dynamometers—it's a real chore to get a reading."

Another thing Heinen managed to overlook is

the rapid deterioration of antipollution devices when cars are on the road. Certainly, it is one thing to have a system which works effectively when the system is brand new and the car is freshly tuned. It is something quite different to have a system which is still effective after months of being clogged and corrupted.

It was precisely this problem which caused the manufacturers to admit, in 1970, that the only way to prevent the rapid destruction of control devices capable of improving on the performance of the devices used in 1968 and 1969 was to ask the oil refineries to stop selling leaded gasoline. This, in turn, would necessitate a major reduction of engine compression levels and an end to the superpowered American car. In other words, the deterioration of control devices, caused largely by the build-up of lead deposits, was such a serious problem that the manufacturers saw no way out of it other than to make major modifications of the internal combustion engine. Of all this, there was not a hint in Heinen's blithe assurances.[29]

The auto industry has never been known for the speed with which it solves the technological or social problems created by its cars. In 1969, the announcement that the war on pollution had been won was absurdly premature, if not blatantly dishonest. Aside from the omissions noted by Barsky, the executives who were willing to have the public relax and stop worrying about car pollution were guilty of an inexcusable deception. The presidents of GM and Chrysler and the vice chairman of Ford were well aware that the control devices they were talking about, the ones they said had "won" the battle, were capable of reducing only two of the three major pollutants emitted by cars. These devices lowered the carbon monoxide and unburned hydrocarbons to "acceptable" levels by raising the combustion temperature. For people who were bothered by carbon monoxide poisoning or chronic emphysema, this was all very well, but through a devilish twist of chemistry, this process failed to reduce the production of oxides of nitrogen; on the contrary, it tended to *increase* it. For people who were bothered by photochemical smog, this was not so good. It will be recalled that oxides of nitrogen are the principal cause of the brownish soup in which the southern half of California is slowly being immersed. Thus, projections made by the Commerce Committee of the Senate in 1968 indicated that if existing control standards were continued, there would be *four times as much* photochemical smog in California's Livermore-Amada Valley in 1998 as there was in 1968, and that the total amount would be 50 percent greater than if there were no controls on cars at all![30]

Even with full (albeit grudging) cooperation from Detroit, therefore, such controls will not solve the pollution problem; they merely subordinate it to a more vexing one—the problem of cost. The simple devices required to meet the lenient standards of 1968 and 1969 were expensive (1968 devices cost

from $20 to $55 per car), but what the manufacturers really feared was the cost of meeting the
more stringent standards of the mid-1970s. In 1968,
it was possible to pass the added cost on to the
consumer, with no measurable reduction of new
car sales, but the cost of meeting projected standards for 1974 or 1975 promised to raise the price
of each car by hundreds of dollars, creating havoc
with both makers ańd consumers. A confidential
study conducted in 1968 by the National Center
for Air Pollution Control projected that emissions
control devices capable of meeting 1975 standards
would probably cost $300 per vehicle in higher
vehicle prices alone. The $300 does not include
added costs of maintenance and inspection and
reduced fuel economy.[31]

The technological limitations of known methods
of exhaust control, combined with the prospect of
prohibitive costs, lent new credibility in the late
1960s to those who claimed the only real solution
to the air pollution problem was to replace the
internal combustion engine.

Hundreds of new engine designs were proposed,
many of which were patently absurd (some rivaled
Cyrano de Bergerac's morning dew balloon for
whimsical ingenuity), and many more of which
were workable in principle but incapable of competing with the internal combustion engine in cost,
size, and performance characteristics. By 1968 it
seemed likely that the eventual successor to the
internal combustion engine, if there was to be any

successor at all, would be either a turbine, an electric motor, or some type of external combustion
engine—most probably a reciprocating steam engine. While the general desirability of these alternatives continued to be debated long after the Big
Three had finally confessed the need for a "look"
at new propulsion technologies, their basic feasibility was already established by the end of the
decade.[32]

At first, interest focused on electric cars. To a
country already accustomed to electric golf carts,
electric elevators, and other electric people-movers,
the idea of an electric car did not strain credulity
(as did, for example, that of a steam car). Electricity connoted modernity and reliability (it was
not only cleaner but quieter), and enthusiasm
mounted rapidly. All over America, men who held
respectable jobs with Bell Laboratories or M.I.T.
by day began building bizarre, electric-powered cars
in their garages by night. Interest filtered up to
the business community, and by 1969 at least
twenty-two companies and one government agency
had produced operational prototypes.[33]

Interest picked up even more when a New York
congressman, Richard Ottinger, began driving an
electric car around his Westchester County neighborhood, preaching the gospel of a cleaner atmosphere. He had gotten the idea while talking
with representatives of the American Public Power
Association (APPA) about air pollution caused by
electric power generators.

"In the course of our discussion," said Ottinger, "they noted that the electric car could provide a possible alternative to the internal combustion engine in the event that effective abatement devices could not be developed. APPA, of course, was interested in this alternative because the recharging of electric vehicles could create an important new market for the commodity they were pushing: electric power. Furthermore, since the recharging would be done at times of minimum demand—at night and during the off-peak day hours—it would help to even out power demand and make generation more efficient. With this in mind, they drafted a bill that was designed to promote research and development of the electric car as a feasible alternative to the internal combustion engine. At this point (September 13, 1966) I introduced the legislation and made speeches on the subject. The response was very encouraging—surprisingly so. I had assumed that people would be cool to the idea of electrics because they had a kind of "horse-and-buggy" image. I feared that insofar as people thought of them at all, they might picture little old ladies driving down the street at the 'daring' speed of 20 mph. I didn't really anticipate that people would understand what we were driving at so quickly."[34]

Ottinger's car, bearing the name Renault Yardney Silvercel, was a public relations triumph. "I suspect that the most dramatic thing that happened to the concept of an electric vehicle alternative was the picture of a congressman commuting to and from the Capitol in a working electric," he recalled.

Other congressmen began to take notice, and in March 1967, Senate hearings were held to study possibilities for replacing the internal combustion engine with an electric car.[35] A caravan of battery-powered cars converged on Washington to demonstrate their drivers' opinions that a replacement was imminently feasible. A transcontinental race between two student-built electric cars came to an embarrassing conclusion when both cars had to be towed to the finish line, but the race was considered a moral victory and interest continued to build. Inevitably, the electric motor industry itself got into the act. Donald C. Burnham, president of Westinghouse, declared that there was a "revolution brewing against pollution, immobility, inconvenience, ugliness, and the rest of the devil's chant of urban woes."[36]

The auto manufacturers, however, were noticeably unimpressed. No electric car, they said, could match the performance of the conventional internal combustion automobile. It was an incontestable point, since none of the vehicles which had been built could exceed 60 mph or go further than 100 miles without stopping to have their batteries recharged.[37] Furthermore, most electric cars provided little or no space for luggage, since the trunk had to be loaded with hundreds of pounds of batteries.[38] It was possible that there would someday be a battery-powered Volkswagen, but there clearly could never be an electric Cadillac.

The manufacturers' reactions were a smoke-screen, however, since the electric car was being envisioned as an urban or commuting vehicle (which could be recharged daily and which would have no need for turnpike speeds) rather than as a replacement for the traditional all-purpose vehicle. It may be argued that only an all-purpose car can satisfy the demands of the average consumer. It can also be argued that these demands put so much strain on cities that the convenience of not having to change vehicles at the periphery of the city is greatly outweighed by the inconvenience of not being able to park or move freely, once the interior of the city is reached. The University of Pennsylvania Department of Electrical Engineering, commissioned by the U.S. Department of Transportation to study the possibilities for an electric car for urban use, concluded in 1968 that such a vehicle could vastly reduce congestion and parking problems. Under the direction of Dr. Manfred Altman, a small but roomy "minicar" was designed and a leasing system devised whereby a commuter would leave his car at a center-city depot in the morning, then pick up another (not necessarily the same) car in the evening. Instead of occupying space in a parking lot during the day, the minicars would be used for a you-drive taxi system. The overall result would be a sharp reduction of the number (as well as the size) of cars converging on the city streets at the same time.

A renewal of the minicar grant provided for the construction of a minicar prototype and eventually for the testing of a fleet of minicars in downtown Philadelphia. But the United States government has had cold feet more than once in its efforts to discipline the auto industry, which views the choking of the cities with remarkable detachment. In 1969, Altman's funds were suddenly and unaccountably cut off. The government, pressed for an explanation, replied tersely that the project had "posed a threat to existing and new mass transit systems in the surrounding areas."[39]

A combination of factors caused attention to shift in 1967 to steam cars. One factor was the disruptive effect conversion to electric cars seemed likely to have on the national economy. Several studies showed that this effect would not be so severe that the country could not endure it, but that it would be considerably more severe than the effect of conversion to a steam car.[40] Steam engines are technically far more similar to internal combustion engines, both in design and in fuel requirements, than are electric motors. Clearly, they would entail much less change. Socially, too, there would be less disruption; people could continue their one-car habits, since steam cars are quite capable of performing at high speeds over long distances. The most significant factor in the broadening of interest from electric to steam power was the pollution issue itself. Whereas electric cars would reduce pollution only in the urban areas where they were used, steam cars used as general-purpose vehicles could produce cleaner air in city and country alike. While it is true that the heaviest air pollution is in the cities, many studies have shown that such pollution has moved to the remotest corners of the countryside as well.[41] The open spaces of America are being increasingly cut and slashed by new highways, and the primary polluter of these spaces, as well as of the cities, is the automobile.

Even if nonpolluting cars were not needed outside the cities, it was argued, the steam car would be a better solution to the pollution problem. The use of electric cars would vastly increase the demand for electric power production, thereby increasing thermal and atmospheric pollution from power plants. According to some experts, little overall reduction of pollution would be gained by such a shift. The steam car, by contrast, converts energy in its own power plant, just as the internal combustion car does. Unlike the internal combustion car, however, it burns its fuel completely instead of ejecting large quantities of unburned fuel into the air.

Old-time steam car "enthusiasts," of course, were aware of these things all along and were among the first to come up with the kinds of innovations required to bring steam car technology sufficiently up-to-date to make it competitive with the modern internal combustion engine. These "tinkerers" (as they were called by Detroit) had little money but lots of faith; many remembered the glory days of the Doble Steamer, which some people still consider one of the finest machines ever built. They were convinced that the internal combustion engine had prevailed, not because of any technological superiority, but because of clever planning by the internal combustion interests, combined with extremely poor management by the steam car manufacturers. Abner Doble, for example, had been an excellent engineer but a notoriously incompetent businessman.

It is no accident, therefore, that in spite of the high cost of developing a new engine, the greatest impetus toward a revival of the steam car in the 1960s came from a pair of small-town backyard mechanics rather than from any of the large automobile manufacturing companies. It was the car built by Calvin and Charles Williams of Ambler, Pennsylvania, which helped convince at least one congressional committee that the return of steam was a reality. On the occasion of the 1968 Hearings of the Senate Commerce Committee, the brothers drove their car to Washington and gave rides to several senators, who were highly impressed with the quick acceleration and smooth, silent ride of the car (steam cars need no transmissions; they accelerate steadily, like a plane, rather than in jerky stages like a car with gears).

Most important, of course, was the nonpolluting quality of the car, dramatically demonstrated in a test conducted by the Mobil Oil Corporation. The Williams car, without any antipollution equipment, was pitted against a brand new Ford. When the results came in, even Henry Ford II had to gulp; the conventional car had produced thirty-seven times as much oxides of nitrogen, forty-five times as much hydrocarbons, and seventy times as much carbon monoxide as the steam car![42] Furthermore, the steam car's emissions levels were so far below the projected standards for 1975 that, as the Commerce Committee observed, "under normal operating conditions, without attempts at emission control, a steam car produces almost no pollution." [43]

The Williams brothers were not the only people working on modernizing steam cars in the 1960s. The concept of a closed-cycle vapor engine, one which would condense and recycle its steam instead of letting it blow away, attracted a number of adventuresome engineers. Several of these, convinced that they had found a technically and economically feasible nonpolluting replacement for the internal combustion engine, raised money and set to work on serious research and development. The auto makers stood by and watched grimly, contributing neither their money nor their know-how to the effort. The coolness with which such research efforts were received in Detroit is illustrated by an exchange of letters between Robert Shaw, Director of Public Relations at General Motors' Harrison Radiator Division, and a Mechanical Engineering class at Carnegie-Mellon University in Pittsburgh. On March 31, 1969, Carnegie-Mellon engineering student Robert Rosenkrantz wrote to Shaw in reference to an earlier conversation, thanking him "for consenting to help my condenser group in its endeavors to design a heat exchanger." He then explained that he and his classmates were planning to use the heat exchanger to build steam engines for marine, bus, and auto applications. After listing several technical problems the class was having, Rosenkrantz noted that a completion date had been set for May 15.

"On 29 May 1969," he concluded, "we will present our findings to government and industry. I should like to extend, at this time, an invitation to you and your staff to attend this all day presentation. Thank you again for your most generous help."

One month later—the day before they had planned to make their final presentation—the students received the following letter:

"We are sorry for the long delay in getting back to you regarding your request for information from Harrison pertinent to the heat exchanger design program you have underway. I returned your call last Friday at the 521-9187 number and again this morning, but there was no answer. The reason for the delay is that careful consideration was given to the information you requested. You will perhaps recall that when you telephoned me first, I asked that you state your questions in a letter so that such consideration could be given. I have since been informed by our Engineering Department that the information you desire is considered to be well within the range of proprietary information as we define it. As a result, I regret that we cannot cooperate with you in this project."[44]

It is curious that General Motors was quite willing to help the students *until* it developed that the heat exchanger would be used to build a steam car. It soon became apparent that General Motors' coolness toward the students' project was not merely an oversight. Others who showed an interest in the possibilities of steam propulsion—and who naturally turned to GM for advice—received the same kind of reaction.

While Detroit was keeping doors firmly closed to further investigation of nonpolluting alternatives, both Congress and the engineering world were growing more and more interested in opening them. In 1968 the Senate Commerce Committee held an extensive hearing on steam cars. Automobile manufacturers, engineers, economists, medical experts, and pollution control authorities were asked to testify. At the conclusion of the study, a staff report summarized the committee's findings in unequivocal terms: *"The Rankine cycle (steam) propulsion engine is a satisfactory alternative to the present internal combustion (gasoline) engine in terms of performance and a far superior engine in terms of emissions."* [45]

This report notwithstanding, the auto manufacturers continued to greet all of the new engines with elaborate scorn. On the subject of electric cars, Henry Ford II announced in 1968 that "we have tremendous investment in facilities for engines, transmissions, and axles, and I can't see throwing these away just because the electric car doesn't emit fumes."[46] The same, apparently, went for turbines, which makers claimed were simply "too expensive to build." When questioned about steam, GM's Roche sniffed that "there is *nothing* in the foreseeable future that is going to be competitive with the internal combustion engine."[47]

When confronted with the fact that pollution control devices simply weren't good enough, the makers began blaming the fuel. "Try using natural gas," they said, as if it had been someone else who had spent all those years persuading the oil industry to make higher and higher octane gasolines. Predictably, the function of this suggestion was to distract critics from the campaign to replace an outmoded engine. Automotive journalists who knew where their bread was buttered latched on to this new idea enthusiastically. Vehicles using such fuels would be "far more practical than the near-quackery concepts, such as electric cars and steam engines, which have been promoted by various interests," wrote one.[48] The natural gas fuel system, it was found, could be adapted to the current engine for a mere $500 to $1500 per car [49] (paid for by the customer, of course), thereby enabling the auto makers once again to rescue their precious engine from the threat of obsolescence.

On those rare occasions when the manufacturers could be persuaded to discuss steam cars on a technical level instead of in scornful generalities, they talked as if they assumed there had been no improvements in such machines since the 1920s. Perhaps such an assumption is understandable, in view of the ingrown nature of the industry. Because Detroit is like one big family in which everyone knows what everyone else is doing, its members undoubtedly fall easily into the habit of assuming that they know everything that is happening in the slumbering world of automotive technology, and in the late 1960s the makers knew darned well that nobody in the fraternity was putting much effort into building a better steam car!

On the other hand, much of what Detroit had to say about steam cars was so absurdly out-of-date that it could only have been intended to exploit public apprehensions—apprehensions which are based on memories of a very different kind of steam car than those which were being built by the Williams brothers and their successors in the 1960s. Modern steam cars are known as "vapor cycle" or "Rankine cycle" engines, but GM chairman Roche, in public interviews, persisted in calling them "steamers"—a term he no doubt had learned as a young man in the 1920s. The earliest steamers had had some important technical shortcomings, such as slow starting time (the water had to be brought to a boil, all at once, as in a kettle) and the need to stop for frequent refills of water. These shortcomings had been subsequently eliminated, but the auto manufacturing industry, blinded by the hubris of oligopolistic dominance, seemed unwilling to recognize that such improvements had ever occurred. (They had been made, to be sure, without any help from Detroit, which was busy spending its enormous "research and development" budget on styling, accessories, and cost-reduction techniques.)

On several memorable occasions, GM's vice president for research, Lawrence Hafstad, was questioned about steam engines in such a way that there was no opportunity for him to duck out by pretending such contraptions had gone out with the horse and buggy. Faced with the chore of discussing external combustion technology as a viable alternative to internal combustion troubles, Hafstad decided to emphasize a point that could not fail to be understood by the most unimaginative listener. The high-pressure steam used to propel steam engines created a "considerable safety hazard," he said. Howard Kehrl, chief engineer of Oldsmobile Division, agreed. "A head of steam is a powerful energy source. With the accent on safety today, would we want 100 million vehicles running around with steam under pressure?"[50] Inevitably, these warnings served to reinforce the fears of those whose imaginations told them that boiler explosions could inflict horrible deaths on the users of steam cars. Because it was tacitly supported by the entire auto establishment, this was a popular view throughout the 1960s. It is vividly illustrated by an editorial which appeared in *Automotive Industries* on April 15, 1968, entitled "Nonsense hits a new Peak":

The latest blast against the automotive industry dished up by the small clique of autoism experts is the accusation that the industry is at fault in having failed to manufacture a new steam powered car. This is a real dandy. It achieves a new peak for organized nonsense. It is to be hoped that such influential senators as Kennedy, Magnuson, Ribicoff, et al, do not get taken in by this gambit of publicity seeking.

When legislators, lawyers, prosecuting attorneys, lobbyists and others who lack modern engineering training attempt to legislate engineering matters, they are moving into an area which is loaded with possibly much more hazard, risk and danger for the public than they realize. Even granting that the hypothetical steam engine could be manufactured, how would Senators Kennedy, Ribicoff and Magnuson, et al, like to be driving down the street behind a steam engine which operates at 3000 psi and 700 degrees F total temperature, and have the engine leak or the boiler leak this superheated steam which could cause such complete physical damage to a human body that even instant death would be more likely than effective first aid?[51]

As it happens, there is another side to this picture. It was quickly supplied by Thomas A. Hosick, a chemist and steam-engine developer of Winston-Salem, North Carolina, who wrote:

> To paraphrase your quality of reasoning, how would Senators Magnuson, Kennedy, and Ribicoff, et al, like to be driving down the street behind an I.C. explosion engine (conventional gasoline engine) which operates on a highly poisonous mixture of obnoxious, toxic gases under 500 psi of pressure and 4000 degrees of searing temperature, while burning a highly volatile and flammable mixture of lead-containing hydrocarbons (gasoline), stored in a tank in twenty-gallon quantities having the explosive potential of 600 pounds of pure nitroglycerine, enough to blow up an entire city block? Neither man or animal would be safe within a quarter-mile of such a machine.
>
> In regard to the nonsense in the preceding paragraph and your "crying wolf" about the modern steam car's explosive potential, the facts are that it just doesn't happen that way. The gasoline car is the more dangerous of the two, but not nearly so hazardous as it could be made out to be. You mention that verification of these facts about the hazards of high-pressure, superheated steam can be obtained from any chief engineer in any local plant. Such "verification," if obtained, would be completely irrelevant to the problem under consideration; the steam power plant engineer is concerned with a system capable of instant release of prodigious quanti-

ties of dangerous steam. The steam car power
plant is incapable of release of steam in a dangerous manner except in the most unusual of
circumstances. Similarly, the conventional gasoline car can release steam in a dangerous manner under unusual circumstances, but it is not
a problem for the careful individual. . . . The
monotube steam generator contains so little hot
water under pressure and that contained is in
such small tubes that a steam explosion, in the
dangerous sense of the word, is an absolute
impossibility. A tubing rupture is no more star-
tling than merely opening a valve to the atmosphere. Although high-pressure 1200-degree
steam can char wood before it expands, after
it expands through an opening it cools very
quickly. I have stood several feet back from a
forceful jet emitting high-pressure, 1200-degree
steam directed on me, and it feels actually like
a cool wind. Such a jet was the entire output
of an automobile-sized steam generator.[52]

In the late 1960s, confronted by such testimony
as this, industry officials—who weren't accustomed
to being contradicted—began to be haunted by their
own equivocation. Offhand comments about steam
engines blowing up, or casual observations that
"nothing" could compete with conventional cars
in the foreseeable future, simply did not make sense
to critical audiences. As available information
about the industry became more widely disseminated, the auto establishment, apparently

determined to continue its policy of keeping opponents and customers off balance, turned to a tactic which took its opponents completely by surprise.

On May 7, 1969, newsmen were invited to the dedication of a new General Motors Research Vehicle Emissions and Safety Laboratory, an impressive event in itself. When they arrived, they were treated to a show designed to make critics blush. One of the critics' main points, of course, had been that for all of its talk about how hard it was trying to solve the problems of congestion and pollution, the industry had produced no significantly new hardware in more than a generation. Now, spread before them on the floor of the new center was the largest quantity of new automotive hardware that had ever been shown at one time. The immediate effect was stunning.

No less than twenty-six new vehicles were on display, and *all* of them were powered by the kinds of unconventional, experimental power plants that experts on air pollution and urban congestion had been wishing for years someone with GM's resources would begin to develop. There were cars powered by "hybrid" (gas-electric) systems, by gas turbines, by liquefied petroleum gas (LPG) engines, by ammonia-fueled engines, by electric motors, and by various external combustion engines. The main attractions were two steam cars, one built by GM Research Laboratories and the other by Besler Developments, Inc., of Oakland, California, under

contract to General Motors. The former, a modified
1969 Pontiac Grand Prix, was described as "the
world's first steam car with complete power accessories, including air conditioning." It may also have
been the world's first steam car with a transmission,
since other builders of steam cars had always considered one of the steam car's principal advantages
to be the fact that none is needed. (GM included
a transmission so that no auxiliary power source
would be required to drive the car's numerous gadgets and accessories while the car was standing
still.)

To those who had grown accustomed to GM's
well-documented antipathy toward steam and
electric cars, the "Progress of Power" show was
rather puzzling at first. However, when they listened to the speeches and read the brochures which
accompanied the display, one disturbing fact began
to become apparent: none of the vehicles worked
nearly so well as comparable vehicles which had
already been built by independent outfits. For each
car, a fact sheet described all the technical
specifications, then ended with a section entitled
"Problem Areas," in which it was made abundantly
clear that despite all the hard work GM Research
Laboratories had been doing on it, and despite the
tremendous progress which had been made, the car
was not *nearly* ready for commercial production
and probably would not be for a long time.[53] The
problem areas for the steam-powered Pontiac, for
example, included Powerplant Size and Weight

("450 pounds heavier than the power plant it replaced, at less than half the horsepower") and Cost
("no cost data is available . . ."), areas in which
the judgment of GM's experts bore little resem-
blance to that of the steam cars' leading developers.
Calvin and Charles Williams, for example, had
demonstrated in a fully operational homemade car
which was actually demonstrated for the Senate
hearings that a steam engine is likely to weigh less,
not more—and by no stretch of the imagination
450 pounds more—than a gasoline engine of comparable power.

There are two possible explanations for the inferior quality of the cars in the Progress of Power
show. One is that GM's research staff was somewhat out of touch with the present "state-of-the-
art" when it built the experimental cars, despite
the fact that the show was billed as an exposition
of the state-of-the-art of new automotive technology. The other is that GM deliberately built and
displayed inferior cars in order to prove a point.
The point, no doubt, is that when GM tells the
public steam cars aren't going to be competitive
with internal combustion cars in the foreseeable
future, the public can rest assured that the big
company knows what it is talking about. As *Automotive News* noted in its May 12 issue, GM
seemed bent on telling the nation's leaders and its
people:

"Look, we are interested in solving the California
and United States auto pollution problems. We've

already done a tremendous amount of work on this problem. We think we know as much, or more, about all the alternative power plants as anyone. But the internal combustion engine is far and away the best answer to our transportation needs."[54]

These tactics are indicative not only of GM's reaction to the anti-internal combustion movement in general, but to innovation in general. The industry had reacted in similar ways, for example, when confronted with a demand for new safety features. Apparently, Detroit saw nothing wrong with this attitude. Until the sharp reassessments of 1970 (highlighted by President Nixon's State-of-the-Union message on pollution and its impact on the quality of life), nobody had ever challenged the industry's methods of promoting its products. Profits had always been the first consideration, and social costs entered into the picture only to the extent that they were good or bad for business. In a sense, since the success of a business is measured in terms of its profit-making capacity, the industry's top officials were only doing what they had been trained to do. Until the end of the 1960s, automobile executives remained thoroughly imbued with the spirit which once motivated General Motors to refuse to buy safety glass for its cars because safety glass would reduce profits. In a letter to GM president Alfred Sloan in 1929, E.I. DuPont had written, "I think General Motors should try to come to a decision as to whether they want safety glass or not." Sloan had promptly replied that "two or three years ago I would have felt that perhaps it was a desirable thing for General Motors to take an advanced position similar to what it did on front wheel brakes, but the way things stand now with our volume increasing ap a decelerated rate, I feel that such a position can not do other than to materially offset our profits."[55]

In 1968 and 1969, the auto industry's use of clever public relations to justify its unwillingness to take "advanced" positions succeeded perfectly—for a while. People really believed that the steam car was a crackpot's dream, that the industry was doing everything in its power to meet its responsibilities, and that the pollution problem was getting solved. When journalists began to grow impatient with the slick assurances of the public relations men, the manufacturers found themselves confronting an increasingly dissatisfied public across a widening credibility gap. But for a time, the antipollution movement played directly into Detroit's hands.

Apologists for the internal combustion engine goaded steam car builders by claiming that such machines could *never* be competitive. William Lear, an accomplished inventor whose imagination had been captured by the challenge of building a totally nonpolluting car, became irked at the smugness of the apologists and decided to prove them wrong. Unfortunately for the cause of the steam car, Lear (who had a great weakness for bravado) responded to this goading with a little goading of his own. Told that his new "delta" steam engine would not work, Lear replied that not only would it work, but he would put it in a racing car and take it to the top of the automotive world in the 1969 Indianapolis 500. Lear had already acquired an impressive record of technical and industrial achievements to back up his claim; it was he who had developed the stereo tape for cars; and his Learjet, a small, fast business jet that the aircraft industry had pooh-poohed, had turned out to be one of the business coups of the decade. His work on the steam racing car was therefore watched with great anticipation by the national press, which was delighted by his colorful personality and immodest claims. He seemed to be to the steam car what Cassius Clay had been to modern boxing, and many people genuinely expected him to sweep the racing world off its feet. When he failed to show up at the track on May 1, it was a crippling blow to the antipollution movement.

Behind the scenes at Lear's Reno, Nevada, laboratories, operations had not been nearly so smooth as Lear's glib prognostications might have suggested. Ken Wallis, Lear's chief engineer, had apparently tried to convince Lear that it was folly to try to build a racer before he had succeeded in building a simple, marketable passenger car. Wallis was an expert race-car engineer—he had helped to design the turbine car which had almost won the Indianapolis in record time two years earlier—and knew what he was talking about. Lear, however, was an impatient man who was accustomed to instant success. He wasn't getting any younger; in fact, a doctor had once pronounced him dead. He had $10 million to spend, and he intended to spend it in the most dramatic fashion possible. For several months, the Lear dynasty seemed destined for glory. Then the money started running out. Wallis left in disgust, and Lear did an about-face. Suddenly he began appearing in the company of Detroit auto officials, claiming that the whole steam idea was ridiculous. In a speech to the Detroit section of the Society of Automotive Engineers in November 1969, Lear said, "I don't see any possibility of adoption of a steam car. No one is going to do it. It is just too complicated. You couldn't find a garage mechanic who could fix one. It is practically unserviceable by the average gas station. I told the federal government this, much to their chagrin. They thought the steam car was the answer to the pollution problem, and I was the savior. But I let them down." [56]

Wallis disagreed, saying that the problem was with Lear rather than with the steam car. Taking several of the Reno engineers with him, he quietly started his own company, Steam Power Systems, Inc., of San Diego. There was no fanfare and no discussion of racing cars. "The trouble with Lear," said Wallis in retrospect, "was that he wanted to jump straight from the drawing board to the race track." What was actually needed, he insisted, was a great deal of careful development—and therefore a great deal of money—culminating in the construction of modest prototypes for passenger cars.

There was one thing about which Wallis was particularly bitter: now that the Lear effort had proved such a fiasco (seeming to reinforce everything claimed by Detroit), money had become extremely difficult to raise. Even the Williams brothers, who shunned publicity and made few claims they couldn't prove with their car, went broke and were forced to abandon any further plans.

Except for his impatience, however, Lear was a miscast from the start. His impatience never caught on with the young generation to whose imaginations President Nixon's vague references to the "quality of life" were intended to appeal. This generation became impatient in its own right, months after Lear's effort stalled, with little awareness either of the reasons for his failure or of the actual possibilities for the future. In some ways a highly romantic generation, the young people of 1970 demanded an end to automotive pollution, just as they demanded an end to Vietnam, without knowing or caring what such a change might cost.

The last months of the decade witnessed a snowballing of events precursing the end of the IC engine and the end of an age in which a "consumer" is one who consumes not only the intended product but also a Pandora's boxful of unintended byproducts. The year had begun with the Justice Department suing the Big Three for conspiring to delay the sale of pollution control devices, and although this suit ended eight months later with a consent decree (equivalent to dropping the case), the heat was on. New York City promptly petitioned the court to require the government to release its findings in the case, and the court agreed. The fallen standard of the Justice Department was quickly picked up by both California and New York State, which accused the auto manufacturers of having withheld pollution control devices since 1953. Similar action was taken by private citizens from coast to coast.

At the same time, faith in the efficacy of such devices was faltering, and interest in alternatives was mounting rapidly. Apparently looking for a comfortable compromise, the auto companies pushed harder at the alternative fuel idea. In October, the General Services Administration, the housekeeping agency for the federal government, converted twelve of its vehicles to a dual fuel system of operating alternately on natural gas and gasoline.[57] In December, California Governor Reagan announced that 175 state cars would be converted to a dual gasoline-natural gas system (at a cost of $400 per car).[58] Work was also hurried on new fuel additives, such as Standard Oil of California's F-310, which was reportedly capable of sharply reducing hydrocarbons.[59] But such compromises were essentially red herrings, since they created as many new problems as they solved—such as prohibitive cost, reduced range, and reduced performance, as well as inadequate reduction of emissions. In an article on the elaborate new antipollution equipment for 1970 cars, *Engineering Opportunities* commented, "Unfortunately, no one feels that this is going to turn the trick. In fact, some people feel that the internal combustion engine may never reach the point in its development where pollution can be adequately controlled, particularly in crowded urban areas."[60] "Some people" apparently included John T. Middleton, commissioner of the National Air Pollution Control Administration, who announced that he had seen "no evidence the motor vehicle industry can meet the standard that is being issued this fall" (for 1971 model cars) without a major overhaul of the IC engine.[61]

All over the country, citizens' groups sprang up like angry mushrooms, determined to end the blight of automotive pollution. Typical of these was a group of George Washington University law students who called themselves GASP (Greater-Washington Alliance to Stop Pollution), and who put their studies into practice by taking legal action against Washington's public buses. These buses, like identical GMC buses everywhere, were emitting so much smoke in 1969 that on one occasion a bus was surrounded by police who thought a bomb had exploded. The bus was merely warming up its engine.

Another group of students, working with faculty members at the University of California (San Diego), began building a 100 h.p. steam engine, sufficient to power a 3000 lb. car at 80 mph. If a group of college students can do it, they said, the auto industry with all its resources should be able to do it, too.[62] At two other universities, MIT and Cal Tech, students announced that a coast-to-coast "Clean-Air Car Race," similar to the Great Electric Car Race of 1968 but open to *any* nonpolluting car, would be held in the fall of 1970.[63]

On December 8, a small group of law students picketed the GM building in New York, charging that the auto industry had reacted with "indifference, venality, and conspiracy" towards efforts to reduce air pollution. At the head of the group was Ralph Nader, who told reporters that this was the beginning of a "nationwide student protest against pollutants." In reference to the aborted Justice Department suit, Nader stated, "Although the case has been settled via a consent decree, the Justice Department's charges that the auto companies and their AMA (Automobile Manufacturers Association) conspired since 1953 to restrain the development and marketing of auto exhaust control systems stand as a reminder of the vast potential for members of this industry *to agree to do nothing.*"[64]

The December 12 issue of *Time,* already on the newsstands, reported that Nader "has never picketed, let alone occupied, a corporate office or public agency." But the times were changing, and, as people grew increasingly impatient, so did tactics. A New York state senator, Edwart T. Speno, announcing the formation of a national committee to search for a nonpolluting vehicle, explained, "We have waited in vain for Washington to do something about producing a true safety car . . . *safe for the people in the environment outside. . . .* We cannot wait any longer." By the end of the year, Washington was ready to acknowledge the task. On Capitol Hill, precursors of a new shift in national priorities had come in the form of a bill designed to create a powerful new economic incentive for producing nonpolluting alternatives to the internal combustion engine (ICE). Introduced jointly by Senator Warren Magnuson and Representatives Thomas Foley and Paul McCloskey on October 27, the bill called for new emissions standards for the sixteen thousand passenger vehicles procured by the federal government each year. As specified in the bill, the standards would be so tough that only a steam or electric car could meet them.[65] The California legislature had just voted on a similar bill—to ban all internal combustion engines in the state after 1975—and although the bill had been defeated (it was passed by the Senate), it was becoming clear that a growing number of legislators were finding ways to cut the apron strings which have always tied the government snugly to the broad lap of the auto establishment.

Within months after the California bill failed, similar measures to ban the ICE by the mid or later 1970s were introduced in the state legislatures of Maryland, Massachusetts, New Jersey, Delaware, New Mexico, Arizona, Washington, Connecticut, and Illinois.[66] California Sen. Nicholas C. Petris, who had introduced the original bill, was already moving on a new tack—preparing legislation that would ban automobiles of *all* kinds in the core areas of nineteen California cities.[67]

On December 17, the Department of Health, Education and Welfare announced the inception of a five-year plan for the development of an alternative to the ICE, noting that the auto industry does not have enough "motivation" to come up with its own new power sources. The Department of Transportation, meanwhile, pursued its own plan for achieving the same purpose. If Detroit could be lured into manufacturing a limited number of Rankine cycle (steam) or other nonpolluting engines (on a subsidized basis, if necessary) by 1974, Department of Transportation officials speculated, the government would then have a strong case for requiring that the industry convert *all* of its production capacity to nonpolluting engines in subsequent years. On December 31, the Department of Transportation received a report from a research firm it had commissioned to study the impact of such a conversion on the American economy. The conclusion of the report was that this conversion could be achieved without causing any major shifts in the input-output structure of the U.S. economy.[68]

On January 1, 1970, President Nixon delivered his first State-of-the-Union speech, in which a dominant theme was that the time to end pollution was "now or never" and that the principal culprit in air pollution was the automobile. The tides of national purpose had shifted rapidly in two years, for in his entire campaign Nixon had never spoken of pollution as an issue. In 1969 GM's Roche had said that nothing could replace the internal combustion engine in the foreseeable future, but by the middle of the following year the whole automotive world knew the unforeseeable had been foreseen.[69]

II—MAKERS

To an American, to live well is to produce well, and the symbol of American productive capacity is the American car. The annual increase of industrial output has become so much of a national habit that, for many Americans, making more cars (or more anything) has become the main reason for getting up in the morning. The fact that some of the things which have suffered as a result of this compulsive push for more and more production might contribute just as much to the national well-being as the things being produced has been largely overlooked in the rush of hurrying off to work each day.

The aura of this institutionalized productivity is so pervasive that, as Eugene Rabinowitz observes in the May 1969 *Bulletin of the Atomic Scientists,* even President Nixon's Secretary of the Interior, Walter J. Hickel—the duly appointed protector of whatever inherent values the air and the land might still be presumed to have—seemed to have been seduced by it. Noting that the secretary had been "arguing for a moderate approach to the prevention of pollution of air and water to avoid slowing down industrial development," Rabinowitz wrote that "for Secretary Hickel (and for many other tradition-minded Americans), industrial development is an *absolute* good, while conservation is only a *relative* one." He then pointed out that what was once a good reason for pushing production is no longer a good reason. "American society (and to a lesser extent, other advanced technological societies as well), are passing from the age of scarcity into the age of plenty. Adequate provision of necessities to all people in this country now depends on better distribution of income and thus, in turn, on a better spread of educational and employment opportunities. It does not, as in the past, depend on increased productive capacity." [70]

The dangers of institutions which have outlasted their functions, especially those whose perpetuation puts heavy demands on the surrounding environment, are epitomized by the production of cars. Whereas some institutions merely ossify with time, like the bones of an old man, others become dangerously malignant. The former die a quiet death, eating out their own vitality until nothing is left but a shell. The latter, however, do not consume their own vitality so much as that of the surrounding environment. Thus, the cult of productivity cannot serve its own ends without sacrificing others. There is nothing wrong with these ends, of course—until in the minds of those who produce or consume they become preeminent. "It is a good thing," says Rabinowitz, "that practically every American has an automobile and can travel across the country in the pursuit of better life, enjoyment, and contemplation of natural beauty. But it is not so obvious that increasing the annual production of automobiles to ten or fifteen million units is desirable, if producing six or eight million is enough to meet the need and to keep workers in the automobile industry adequately employed.

"If this increase in production requires artificial stimulation of demand by appeals to vanity, by capital investment in superficial but price-increasing alterations (not to speak of reducing the strength and mechanical durability of automobiles to accelerate their obsolescence), further increase in automobile production from year to year is not an unmitigated 'good.' It may well be more of an evil. It uses up irreplaceable raw materials, such as metals and oil, more rapidly than necessary. It chokes the streets of American (and European) cities, until it becomes faster to walk than to drive, only nobody wants to walk, even if it is faster! Too many automobiles, fed annually into the nation's system, may be as bad for national health as too many steaks, pizzas or potato chips fed into the organism of an individual."

In a production-oriented society, the king of corporations is that one which can produce the most. General Motors Corporation, with the largest manufacturing capability and greatest revenues of any corporation in the world, has acquired a special mystique. What GM has come to be is not so much a company as a whole nation unto itself.[71] Its net operating revenues, said *Fortune* in 1966, "last year exceeded the gross national product of all but nine nations in the free world." [72] GM's net sales total some $20 billion per year, including about $1 billion worth of military contracts.[73] Its financing subsidiary, General Motors Acceptance Corporation (GMAC), is the single largest seller of short-term commercial paper in America, with outstandings rivaling the United States Treasury itself.[74]

Speeches by General Motors executives are richly laced with the cliches of production. Implicitly, the superiority of the American way of life is equated with the superiority of the American productive capacity. In a typical James Roche speech, the same theme is pounded home again and again: "To trade with other nations and to protect our markets at home, our industry must be competitive. To be competitive we must be productive. . . . We must maintain and improve productivity. . . . When people are nonproductive through no fault of their own, we must provide the means by which they can be made productive. . . . The problems of the nonproductive and disadvantaged are not confined to the cities." [75]

The power of General Motors is viewed by the rest of the country with very mixed feelings. For middle America, GM is more a thing of legend—like the most powerful football team in the world, or the most dangerous gang—than a real threat. If Hollywood were to make a movie about GM, the very last line of the film could be taken directly from a speech James Roche made at the Dayton Golden Moments Dinner (at the National Cash

Register Company) on September 12, 1968. "Today," said Roche (in the movie, he could be played by John Wayne), "we hear a lot about bigness—bigness in government, bigness in labor, bigness in business. Some who think small would have us think bigness is bad. But America is a big country in a big and very competitive world. And today, if we are to think ahead, we must think big." [76] It is no wonder that for nearly a quarter of a century college students have debated the question of "breaking up General Motors," along with such other basic questions as whether there is a God and who will win the World Series.

The mystique of General Motors has had a curious effect on the company's relationship to the country which spawned it. GM not only epitomizes the qualities of size and power with which it has endowed its cars; it is in some senses a microcosm of the American state. Like the United States, it is the richest, most potent, most influential entity of its kind. It is in many ways responsible for the well-being of other companies, yet it is also in the position of having to compete with them. Like the United States, it has the power to destroy its competition and must use considerable restraint to avoid doing so. Also like the United States, it has often succumbed to the temptations of power, impinging on its competitors in ways which have been called everything from "ruthless exploitation" to "protecting its interests."

Quite aside from its enormous political clout, the

fact that GM is a kind of monument to American virtues has enabled it to maintain a snug relationship with the government which is supposed to regulate it. There is a thick bond of understanding between the men who run the federal bureaucracy and those who run the Big Three. Both have closed their doors against popular clamors they do not understand. As Roche observed in a speech before the Illinois Manufacturers Association in 1968, "Business and government can ill afford to be adversaries. So mutual are our interests, so formidable are our challenges, that times demand our strengthened alliance. . . . Today, business and government are each becoming more involved in the affairs of the other." [77]

On another occasion, Roche was more specific about the nature of these challenges. Speaking at a "prayer breakfast" held by Chicago's Mayor Richard Daley in 1969, Roche spoke grimly and repeatedly of the need for "law and order." Apparently, Roche was as upset about young people accusing the industrial establishment of "indifference, venality, and conspiracy" toward efforts to reduce pollution, as Daley was about young people accusing the political establishment of indifference to the changing face of American politics. The distinction between public and private sectors was in many ways less important now than distinctions between styles of life.

The bonds which tie government and big business are in many ways closer than those which tie big business and small business. Seekers of jobs and favors move easily from Washington to Detroit, and vice versa, bringing with them lasting friendships and loyalties. A president of General Motors, Charles Wilson, becomes secretary of defense. He brings with him his vice president, Roger Kyes, to be deputy secretary; later Kyes returns to GM as vice president and director. A president of Ford, Robert McNamara, becomes *another* secretary of defense. A ranking member of the State Department, Thomas Mann, becomes president of the Automobile Manufacturers Association. A president of American Motors, George Romney, becomes secretary of housing and urban development. A former secretary of commerce, John T. Conner, becomes a director of General Motors. Walter Mote, the brother of Automobile Manufacturers Association lobbyist Lynn Mote, becomes an administrative assistant to Vice President Spiro Agnew.

Corporation lawyers for General Motors are repeatedly recruited from the Antitrust Division of the Justice Department. Law firms representing GM release young associates for public service to antitrust chiefs and deputy chiefs. After several years of on-the-job training, the young associates go right back to work for GM—as legal counsel.[78] The connections are endless. Those who wield power in Washington and Detroit are "in bed together," as a Department of Transportation official put it in 1970.[79] And much of America is excluded from their bed, for reasons that are quite obvious.

An automobile commercial shows a man, expensively and conservatively dressed, striding purposefully through an airport. He moves quickly; people defer admiringly. He has a ruthless look. "This man has power . . . and knows how to use it," says the voice. He steps into his waiting car and drives off. No one will mistake this man for the neighborhood grocer. We think: this man is a big wheel, either in big business or the government. We are supposed to envy this man, and we do. But if we are restless students or small businessmen, we think of him as different, as someone on the other side. It is not a matter of politics. We know that Republicans lean one way and Democrats another, but this man could be either. It is not Republicans and Democrats so much as the powerful and the powerless who represent the opposing interests in an increasingly polarized America. Agencies of government, such as the Justice Department and the Federal Trade Commission, are supposed to regulate the excesses of private enterprise, but this regulation is rarely more severe than the coddling of a precocious child by a mother who fears that the sting of discipline will stunt her child's growth. The bigger the business, it seems, the more coddling it gets.

But General Motors has more foresight than to rely on coddling. Its alliances extend to other big businesses, as well as to the federal government. Most members of GM's board of directors are unknown to the public, but in the labyrinths of business they wield enormous power. In 1968, sixteen members of the GM board held directorships in seventy-six companies, including AT&T, U.S. Steel, IBM, Mobil Oil, Gulf Oil, Aluminum Company of America, Uniroyal, and M.I.T. Some of the directorships are in industries—such as railroads—with which the auto industry directly competes.[80]

According to Ralph Nader, the omnipresence of GM is illustrated by the futile attempts of Calvin and Charles Williams to get financing for their steam car, which posed a threat to GM's conservative interests. Despite the fact that the brothers had demonstrated their car to be a viable and potentially lucrative alternative to the internal combustion car, no banks were willing to back their research. Although there is no evidence of any conspiracy (both Nader's and the Williams' claims notwithstanding), it is interesting to note that General Motors has a powerful influence in the banking community, and GM representatives are readily available to speak with bank officials who need to determine the advisability of financing new undertakings in the automotive field. Members of the General Motors board of directors hold directorships with Morgan Guaranty Trust Company, First National Bank of New York, First National Bank of St. Louis, Mellon National Bank and Trust Company, American Fletcher National Bank and Trust Company, St. Louis Union Trust Company, First National Bank of Boston, the National Bank of Detroit, the Royal Bank of Canada, and the

Montreal Trust Company,[81] to cite examples.

In any case, the fortunes of General Motors have been so tied to those of the country at large that government agencies have rarely made any serious attempts to regulate the company's activities. Law enforcement, when applicable to GM, often breaks down. In 1969, California Deputy Attorney General Charles O'Brien wrote: "The lack of faith in our system of government stems in great part from our failure to achieve justice and equality in our law. Mary Mammary dances in a bar without wearing a blouse and her little brother Winston accepts a marijuana cigarette from a friend. The answer of the law is swift and sure and the penalties severe. General Motors puts phony prices on its cars and enters into agreements to slow up smog control. Other industries pollute our water and poison our air. In these cases, the wheels of justice grind slowly—if at all." [82]

In the area of antitrust violations, the record is very similar. Sen. Gaylord Nelson, chairman of the Monopoly Subcommittee of the Small Business Committee, noted in 1968 that "There has been only one case in which the antitrust enforcement authorities have ever attacked monopoly (as opposed to other antitrust activities) in the passenger car manufacturing industry proper. There the defendant was Checker, which about twenty years ago was charged with monopolizing the market for taxicabs in a half-dozen cities." [83] A list of other antitrust actions brought by the U.S. against GM

between 1930 and 1968—most of them alleging conspiracy to restrain trade—shows that the company
was actually acquitted only three times in seventeen cases; yet few Americans can remember ever
seeing GM humiliated by publicity about its monopolistic practices. Examination of the antitrust
record shows that the largest fine GM ever had
to pay was a few thousand dollars (the exact
amount, according to the Justice Department, was
$56,200—and that heavy burden was shared with
several other corporations!).[84] To a driver who has
lost control of his car and injured another person,
such a fine might constitute serious punishment
(though personal liability awards are often larger),
but to a company whose annual sales exceed the
combined general revenues of the state and local
governments of New York, New Jersey, Pennsylvania, Ohio, Delaware, Connecticut, Rhode Island,
Vermont, New Hampshire, Massachusetts, and
Maine, a fine of five or ten thousand dollars is not
even a gentle reprimand. More often than not, the
government's cases against GM have ended in quiet
"consent" decrees, amounting to a promise by the
defendant to "go and sin not." [85]

For people who are frustrated with the slowness
and awkwardness of democratically responsible institutions, the efficiency of General Motors is a
thing to be envied. GM requires no public mandate
for its policies, even though these policies affect
people's lives as much as do those of governments.
It is subject to no real controls by its stockholders,

whose votes have never succeeded in overriding the wishes of the directors. Consequently, it has been able to mobilize its assets with a degree of effectiveness rarely achieved by the United States itself. Even such nonauthoritarians as Arthur Okun, chairman of the Council of Economic Advisers under President Lyndon Johnson, have confessed to being awed by GM to such an extent that they would be extremely reluctant to lay a hand on it. Okun recalled playing a game with his fellow economists, in which they asked themselves the question, "If you had a button you could push and GM would be instantly broken up, would you push it?" Okun said he agonized over the question but finally decided he would not push the button.[86]

Others would push such a button without hesitation. GM's lack of responsibility is distressing to many who are concerned about the diminishing control of the individual citizen over the course of his own life. This is a society in which social progress is slow, even when the administrating government is answerable to all citizens. When a pseudopublic body as large as General Motors is *not* legally answerable, its effects on social justice can be devastating.[87]

Some of these effects are felt within the manufacturing organization itself, in such matters as the awarding of retail franchises. Auto executives miss no opportunities to mention that their Negro employment is proportional to the number of Negroes in the United States, but they do not mention what kinds of jobs these Negroes hold. It is convenient for a manufacturer to hire the people who live near his plants. The proportion of Negroes living in the depressing environment created by Detroit's factories—largely because they are too poor to escape—is far higher than the national average. However, in the business of retailing new cars, a black dealer is as hard to find as a Quaker police chief, despite the fact that financing is readily available (from GMAC) to would-be franchisees who have no money of their own to invest. In 1968 there were thirty thousand dealers in the United States, of whom four were black.[88]

The most mysterious aspect of GM's power is its domination of the auto-manufacturing industry. Domination is by nature hard to demonstrate, since it can take a variety of ambiguous forms, not all of which are visible to the casual observer. Pre-Revolutionary Russians had little awareness of the extent of Rasputin's influence over the Czarina. GM's hold on Chrysler and Ford is an equally insidious one. Economists have noted, for example, that prices on new cars are invariably set by GM and followed slavishly by the other makers. All of the makers argue that this is only evidence of intense price competition. Indeed, it is true that the symptoms of perfect competition and those of perfect collusion are strangely similar. As Brown University economist Mark B. Schupack testified in Senate hearings in 1968, "Similar prices can imply a perfectly collusive cartel as well as a perfectly competitive market." [89] While the significance of similar prices *per se* may be ambiguous, there is a considerable difference between lowering prices to meet the competition, and *raising* them. On at least one occasion, Ford has announced its prices before General Motors, then changed its mind when GM announced prices higher than Ford's. Instead of taking competitive advantage of its own previously advertised prices, Ford bashfully raised its prices to match those of its "rival."

The pattern of General Motors setting the pace while the other companies trot faithfully along at its heels has not been limited to pricing. In the area of automotive engineering, Ford and Chrysler have steadfastly refused to strike out on their own. The fact that the "other two" of the Big Three rarely try anything new until GM tries it first cannot be interpreted as the inability of smaller companies to outstrip a larger competitor. On the contrary, Chrysler and Ford have been known to "sit" on their ability to make a particular improvement for years, until GM gives the signal to incorporate it into the American car. For example, disc brakes were used on European cars for years before they ever crept onto an American car. Ford and Chrysler could easily have gained a leg on GM by using them, yet refused to do so until GM "introduced" them in the 1960s.[90]

No one claims that there is *no* competition in the auto industry, but there is strong evidence that the bulk of competition lies in those areas which

the public sees—the retail market—while the manufacturing end of the operation has become primarily
a cooperative affair. When it comes to public policy,
the manufacturing companies often speak with a
single voice. In November 1968, a new rule providing for increased consumer information was proposed by the National Highway Safety Bureau.
The usual procedure, in cases where companies are
affected by a proposed rule change, is for all interested parties to submit their individual views pending a final decision. In this case, there were no
responses from GM, Ford, or Chrysler. Instead, the
Automobile Manufacturers Association submitted
a statement in behalf of the individual companies.
Despite the complexity of the issue, the statement
indicated not only that the Big Three held common
views on every detail, but that they had gotten
together to decide on their policy as easily as if
they were simply three divisions of a single corporate body.[91] Such getting-together is not normally characteristic of competitive entities.

In the same year, a Detroit journalist discovered
that two different auto executives had given an
identical speech on the subject of air pollution.
What bothered the journalist was not that two
speakers were content to use the same words, but
that one of the executives happened to be from
Ford and the other from GM. Writing in the *Detroit
News,* he noted that "the auto industry is supposed
to be one of the most highly competitive in the
world. Obviously, the competition ends at the

speaker's platform." [92] There is other evidence.

On another occasion, the student newspaper at the University of Michigan came up with a curious item. It claimed that the Big Three had drafted a secret financial assistance plan, according to which if one company was struck the other two would reimburse it for 40 percent of the production it lost during the strike. A photo of the alleged document was printed in the paper. GM, of course, vigorously denied the whole thing, despite the fact that the heading on the document indicated that it had come from GM's own cost analysis section. [93]

These phenomena, however, are only the symptoms of abnormality; they do not explain why, in an economy where people expect rival enterprises to try to outdo each other, the makers of automobiles merely march together in lockstep. The apparent explanation for this behavior lies in the unusual concentration of the industry. Taken to its ultimate extreme, concentration is monopoly. The auto industry is the most highly concentrated industry in the United States (other than the government-controlled utilities), with four companies accounting for 99.9 percent of all production and one company—[eneral Motors—accounting for about 55 percent. That this represents an extreme distortion of the normal market structure is reflected in the unaccountable discrepancy between the Justice Department's guidelines for antitrust enforcement and the actual situation prevailing in Detroit. According to guidelines made public on

May 30, 1968, the Justice Department will generally challenge mergers between two firms, each of which account for 4 percent of a highly concentrated market. "Such a challenge," says Ralph Nader, "would presumably be grounded on Justice's belief that the new firm possessing 8 percent of a highly concentrated market would have an effect, to use the language of Section 7 of the Clayton Act, 'to substantially lessen competition or to tend to create a monopoly.' And yet General Motors, with its staggering 50 to 55 percent of the market, finds itself immune from antitrust enforcement aimed at its monopolistic structure." [94]

Auto magnates dismiss the concentration of their industry with a wave of the hand. In one press release, GM noted that "there are good economic reasons for such large size. One reason is that automobiles can not be produced in the volume essential to low cost without large investment in plant, equipment, machinery, and specialized tools. . . . A second reason is the breadth of the market. Because of the mobility of the automobile, sales, service and replacement parts must be available throughout the country." [95]

Interestingly, this completely contradicts a statement made by General Motors president Harlow Curtice in a Senate Judiciary Committee hearing several years earlier. Asked by the committee "why it is necessary for General Motors to be as large as it is from the standpoint of economic efficiency," Curtice promptly replied, "I do not think that the size has anything to do with it." [96]

Nor do the administrators of today's auto industry explain why, if American Motors is large enough to produce, market, and service several lines of cars throughout the country at GM's prices, GM must be twenty times the size of American Motors. Of course, it should be noted that American Motors makes very little profit, certainly much less per car than GM. In fact, there is some evidence that GM, Ford, and Chrysler are helping to keep American Motors alive just to prove that other companies can compete with the Big Three if they wish. As Nader pointed out in a 1968 Senate hearing, American Motors Corporation would probably have dropped out of the auto business several years ago "were it not for special tax relief and reliably reported assistance by GM as supplier and general benefactor." [97] All of this merely shows that the makers have a certain proclivity for doubletalk, claiming on one hand that giant size is necessary for efficient production, while insisting on the other hand that such size is not necessary for new companies entering the market.

In any case, the efficiency "argument" is a weak excuse for the enormity of GM and Ford, because the various manufacturing divisions of these companies operate somewhat independently of each other (in making cars, as distinguished from policy), and most of these divisions are not much bigger than American Motors. For economies of scale, apparently, there is a curve of diminishing returns.

In a definitive study of economies of scale, Joe S. Bain concludes that an optimal plant complex in the auto industry would be one designed for between 300,000 and 600,000 units per year—only slightly more than the output of American Motors, and far smaller than that of Chrysler, the smallest of the Big Three.[98]

On the other hand, it is equally specious to argue that American Motors' presence proves that the industry is wide open to new competition. In a country where technology and business have both boomed, it is strange that the automotive industry has become barren ground for new enterprises. There have been hundreds of producers of automobiles in the past half-century of American history, but today there are only four. Where have the others gone? If American Motors finds its pastures so green, why does no other company join it in competing with the Big Three? Americans have a passion for science and a tradition of free enterprise that should have the auto industry teeming with new activity of social and environmental significance. Instead, the industry has remained virtually dormant for two decades. There must be a reason why, in a land of rampant growth, the automobile business has become a technological wasteland. The most visible effect of this industry's concentration is the pall of sameness it casts over its products and the easy temptation it offers its members to form quiet, profitable conspiracies at the expense of its consumers. "Despite high profits which, theoretically, should have attracted new entrants to the market, the auto industry has failed to attract a single new domestic competitor in recent years," says Louisiana State University economist Sidney Carroll. "Clearly, then, enormous disadvantages, apparently considered insuperable by potential entrants, must confront the would-be manufacturer." [99]

Coming from GM, there is something very persuasive about the argument that if tiny American Motors Corporation can compete in the auto market, so can anyone else. However, while AMC is certainly tiny by comparison with GM, it is actually a very large company by absolute standards; on *Fortune*'s 1968 list of the 500 largest industrial corporations in the United States, AMC ranked 113th.[100] Yet American Motors has still had trouble competing with the established names of GM, Ford, and Chrysler—and *not* because it is too small to achieve necessary economies of scale.

Apparently, the "name" is an almost unsurmountable obstacle for a new competitor. Everybody is familiar with Ford, GM, and Chrysler, but relatively few Americans know anything about AMC, and many have "never heard of it." Auto makers claim that the consumer is very knowledgeable about the product he buys and is quite able to choose intelligently among the models offered by the different firms. Bain disagrees, pointing out that in the case of the automobile (as distinguished from some other products), the consumer cannot judge the quality of the product he buys but must rely upon the reputation of the manufacturer. "The passenger car is a large complex mechanism, so complex that the average buyer (though he may not quite admit it) is quite unequipped to evaluate its mechanical design and its general level of quality." [101] This reputation is built up over a period of time through heavy advertising (GM's advertising bill is about $240 million per year) [102] and other sales promotion devices. Big Three products also get millions of dollars worth of free advertising through their dealer networks. The establishment of such a reputation is the price of admission to the world's most exclusive private club.[103]

In this connection it is interesting to note that all of the Big Three have been spending millions of dollars to consolidate their company names. In 1966, GM began using its "Mark of Excellence" signs as a way of sharpening public recognition of Chevrolet, Buick, Oldsmobile, Pontiac, and Cadillac as GM products. Fourteen thousand signs were scheduled to be replaced (over a ten-year period) at a cost of $275 million.[104] The costs of similar programs at Ford and Chrysler were reputed to be $110 million and $65 million respectively. With that kind of money being spent on signs alone, it would be hard for any new name to sound anything but obscure—and highly suspect—to the consumer.

The auto makers find their situation a particularly comfortable one, not only because they have little to fear from outside competition at the manufacturing level, but also because they have less and less to fear from the supplying and purchasing levels as well. To a large extent, the makers of cars purchase parts and materials not from independent companies but from their own subsidiaries. General Motors is its own supplier for hundreds of items required for the manufacture of cars, including everything from pig iron to stereo tape decks.[105]

Companies in the automobile industry at large (including parts manufacturers) spend more money on purchases from their own sector (i.e., from their own subsidiaries or from other auto or parts manufacturing companies) than they do from the steel, rubber, glass, plastic, electrical equipment, and tool manufacturing industries *combined*.[106] The auto industry is often praised for its contribution to the national economy, but no one mentions how much of the money it generates the industry simply keeps for itself. Whereas most American industries contribute $7 to the Gross National Product for every $1 they spend within their own sector, the auto industry actually spends more on its own sector than it adds to the Gross National Product.[107] In other words, auto companies have much less need to go outside their own industry to conduct business than have most other companies.

In effect, the automobile industry is a whole economy-within-the-economy, and its fiscal policies are decided in the administrative offices of General Motors, for GM is a major supplier not only to its own factories but to those of Ford, Chrysler, and American Motors. It is also the primary market for scores of specialized parts manufacturers. Naturally, other companies depend on it heavily, both as a supplier of products which cannot easily be obtained elsewhere and as a purchaser of products which cannot easily be sold elsewhere.

One effect of such an elaborately integrated arrangement is to put a "price squeeze" on smaller companies which cannot afford to own their own private shopping centers. This is done by narrowing the margin between a raw material price and a finished-good price to a point where the integrated firm still makes a profit but the nonintegrated firm does not—or makes a much smaller one. GM, for example, is capable of narrowing the margin either by lowering the prices of its cars or by raising the prices (to its competitors) of its parts.[108] GM's profit margin is significantly higher than those of its competitors, although Ford and Chrysler still make fat profits and still seem to follow the policy that the Big Three are stronger together than apart. All three are sufficiently integrated to enjoy the benefits of squeezing smaller companies.

All this concentration of economic power has a crushing effect on the people who drive cars. There was a time, presumably, when manufacturers decided what to build on the basis of what the customer said he wanted. In the modern auto industry, the manufacturers first decide what to build, then how to make the customer want it. With corporate planning replacing competition as the principal determinant of the product, the old process of supply-and-demand is short-circuited. The customer no longer has the power he once had to get the product he once got by inducing different producers to vie for his patronage. Among the concrete manifestations of the consumer's waning influence are higher costs (both of purchase and of repair), poor quality, and technological obsolescence. Desired improvements fail to materialize,[109] while changes, for which the customer never asked, proliferate.

It is also painfully evident that the makers have little motive for technological innovation or improvement. Despite the impressive frequency with which Detroit has announced new safety features since the Nader embarrassment of a few years ago, the accident rate has failed to diminish significantly. In 1968, automobile accidents claimed 55,500 people, an increase of almost 50 percent over the 38,000 who died in 1961. This increase could *not* be accounted for by the expanding population of the country, since the number of deaths per 100,000 population rose from 20.8 in 1961 to 27.8 in 1968.[110] According to Federal Highway Administrator Frank C. Turner, the number of people injured in car accidents every five days in 1968 was equal to the number of men wounded in the Vietnam War during that entire year. About *ten thousand* persons are injured *every day,* including about one thousand who are stabbed by superfluous structures on the front ends of cars.[111] The direct annual cost to the nation of all this damage was estimated by the Department of Transportation to be more than twenty-five billion dollars. In 1969 the toll was even higher. The highways of America have become a kind of never-ending demolition derby, with some fourteen million crashes taking place each year.[112] This does not include a large number of accidents other than crashes, such as the one in which the young son of Detroit Mayor Jerome Cavanaugh was nearly strangled by a rear power window.

The auto makers have made tremendous public relations mileage out of very little fundamental change. They are fond of saying that today's cars are safer than ever before. These claims are not exactly untrue, but they are, in their general effect, highly misleading. Improvements in safety, like those in pollution control, are more rhetoric than reality. As Jack Anderson wrote in his "Washington Merry-Go-Round" column in November 1969, "The big auto makers have been dazzling car buyers with glittering sales promotion about new safety features. But in the backrooms of the Senate, the car companies are lobbying furiously to sabotage the federal auto safety law."

One target of the lobbyists in 1969 was a proposal by Sen. Vance Hartke of Indiana to increase the staff of the National Highway Safety Bureau from 518 people to 670. The Highway Safety Bureau is responsible, not only for figuring out how to make cars safer for people when they happen to collide, but also for figuring out how to prevent collisions in the first place. Its responsibilities range from psychological research to highway engineering, and it is ludicrously understaffed (the United States employs more people to hold doors for generals' wives than it does to improve automobile safety). Yet, according to Anderson, the auto industry was "desperately trying to head off" Hartke's reform.[113]

The industry's irreverence for the National Highway Safety Bureau is evident: Detroit does not like to have its hands tied by anyone, and the NHSB has threatened to dictate more and more of what the makers may or may not do. The makers' opposition to expanding the bureau is a blatant example of corporate bad citizenship, particularly in view of the bureau's desperate inability to keep up with the mounting trouble on the country's highways.

The nature of this trouble is illustrated by the plight of the good old yellow school bus, a vehicle some people remember for its frustrating reliability. In the old days, the school bus never missed a day of school, much as the kids, who were somewhat more vulnerable, sometimes wished it would. Since the mid-1960s, however, the school bus has apparently become much less dependable. On September 2, 1969, a Washington, D.C., school bus operator, John Donovan, went to High Point, North Carolina, to pick up three brand new GM school buses he had ordered. On the way back to Washington, Donovan and his drivers were forced to stop *twelve times* for repairs. During the next three months, the buses proved to be so shabbily built that the operator had to spend 225 hours either making repairs himself or hauling the buses to a shop to be repaired. This came out to two hours a day, seven days a week. It also cost Donovan over $1000 in cash, even though each of the three buses had traveled less than six thousand miles. Donovan had had other GMC buses before and had not been dissatisfied. But the new '69s were so bad that Donovan became reluctant to use them lest he endanger the lives of children.[114]

His experience was no fluke. Billy Jubb, owner of the Jubb Bus Company of Pasadena, Maryland, said "I've been in the bus business a long time, but these four '69 GMs are the worst I've ever owned. Each has had a broken bell crank on the clutch. On top of that, I'm always taking the damn things to the dealer to have them adjusted." Another owner, Thomas Gist of Sykesville, Maryland, said "In twenty-five years of operating school buses, I've had more trouble with these two—plus a '68—than all others combined." (Gist's buses, too, were made by General Motors).

In Fairfax County, Virginia, the brakes on a brand new '69 GM school bus failed and the bus finally came to a stop in a pasture. The year before, a new '68 GM belonging to the same owner had its brakes fail while carrying eighteen children. In Huntsville, Alabama, a school bus crashed when its brakes failed, and a boy was killed. In March

1969, General Motors, which makes most of the school buses in America, recalled ten thousand school buses for defective brakes. In February 1969, several thousand more were recalled. A testimony to the deadening effect of monopoly on product quality and innovation was provided by Dr. William Haddon, former director of the National Highway Safety Bureau, who told a reporter that school bus design had shown "virtually no major improvement in the last thirty or forty years." And Haddon was well aware that the NHSB couldn't do a thing about it (the bureau couldn't afford more than one full-time expert on school bus safety standards).[115] Yet the auto industry, while making more and more messes for the bureau to clean up, was lobbying heavily to prevent the bureau from getting more help!

Schoolchildren are not the only victims of heel-dragging in the auto industry. In 1969, General Motors suddenly postponed a previously announced plan to install headrests on all its cars, due to what it called "competitive pressures." [116] In 1968, the Big Three had tried to force the government to abandon some of its safety standards demands.[117] Earlier, they had lobbied vigorously against seatbelts.[118] Another kind of heel-dragging was keeping progress in the development of new urban transportation systems at a virtual standstill. The power of reaction in this area is demonstrated by the activities of the "freeway" interests in northern California, where twenty lobbyists were hired—one at a salary of $106,000—to prevent any diversion of tax funds from highways to mass transit.[119] It is also demonstrated by the grotesquely distorted budget of the U.S. government, which spends $750 million per year for tobacco subsidies, but only $27 million for the safety work of the National Highway Safety Bureau.[120] In 1969, as a result of auto and highway clout, the federal government spent $50 on highways for every dollar it spent on mass transit.[121]

To the extent that any real improvements in safety and quality have been made, they have been almost exclusively gadget-oriented. The fact that there is a desperate need for fundamental new systems and designs seems to have no bearing on the industry's course. The policy seems to be that if changes must be made, these changes are going to have to be very, very profitable. The proliferation of gadgets required to meet tougher safety and pollution standards fits nicely into the old scheme of making fat profits on accessories and replacements. Thus, in 1968 the industry soothed its hurt at having to produce shoulder harnesses by charging the customer *ten times* what they cost to make.[122]

Obliviousness to social and technological change has characterized auto-making policies in nearly every area but style. For annual style changes, extravagant sums are spent. In 1961, the costs for model changes alone totaled $679 million.[123] Nader has estimated that this works out to about $700 per car![124] By comparison, very little has been spent to make cars safer, more practical, or more reliable than they were thirty years ago. "The lead-acid battery was used in the Model-A Ford, and although we have a better one, it is still a lead-acid battery in the sleekest and most expensive car," said Gordon D. Friedlander of the Burndy History of Science Library in Norwalk, Connecticut, in 1969.[125] "Traction, despite the vast increase in power, has not materially improved in forty years. The fourteen-inch wheels (the result of the stylists' mania for an ever-lower profile) afford far less tractive torque, and far more wear, than the old eighteen-inch wheels.

"The cooling systems on most cars are still 'bubble, bubble, boil and trouble,' summer and winter. Although a number of aircraft engines had sealed, chemical-cooled systems in the 1920s, using diethylene glycol as the coolant, this design was not incorporated in car designs."

In the safety area, some progress was brought about by the enactment of new federal standards under the Motor Vehicle Safety Act of 1966, which requires that manufacturers notify owners of any "defect" which "relates to safety." However, such standards are easily compromised, as was illustrated by the incredible truck wheel case of 1969.[126] On May 26, General Motors issued a warning that the wheels on GMC's 1960-1965 three-quarter ton trucks were constructed in such a way that they sometimes fell apart when the truck was overloaded. Unfortunately, the warning came four to nine years too late; the National Highway Safety Bureau promptly reported that it knew of more than seventy cases in which GMC's three-piece disc wheels had split and that at least twenty injuries had occurred as a result. The bureau had "prompted" GM to issue the warning, but the company adamantly disclaimed any responsibility and insisted that owners replace the wheels at their own expense. The key to the GM claim was the "defect" clause of the Motor Vehicle Safety law. Asserting that the wheels were "not defective," the GM statement suggested that failures were usually caused by the extra weight of a camper or trailer. However, the fact that both GM and its dealers had suggested the possible use of trailers and campers in their advertising campaigns for these vehicles was interpreted by some critics as evidence that wheels which could not withstand such weights were defective indeed.

There can be little doubt that the overall quality of cars has declined. In 1968, the four manufacturers recalled 30 percent of their cars.[127] Even this doesn't adequately reflect the magnitude of the problem. Some of the vehicles which were not recalled were even worse than the ones which were. For example, there were the 123,017 Army M151 jeeps built by Ford (the present owner of the once-famous Willys), in which thousands of soldiers had been injured and killed in a series of freakish accidents (who needs war?). The M151, it seemed, had the same "oversteer" problem the Corvair had. Wheels tended to slide away from the direction of a turn, even at low speeds, often causing a vehicle to roll over unexpectedly. In 1967, these jeeps killed 104 soldiers and injured 1,858. While only 1.6 percent of all domestic accidents normally involve turnover, 36 percent of the jeep mishaps did.[128]

Domestic cars were showing their poor quality in other ways, however. In 1968 the Highway Safety Bureau revealed that at least nineteen models had failed to meet its minimum safety requirements, including eight models which flunked the brake test.[129] In the same year, *Consumer Reports* noted that "this year's Chevrolet Chevelle Wagon had the longest list of serious problems we have recorded in any car *ever*." [130] In 1969 and 1970, there was no discernible improvement. Dr. Martin Stern of Washington, D.C., the owner of a new 1969 Mercury, was naturally distressed when the accelerator pedal fell off at 65 mph for the second time in the few weeks he had had the car. Seeking an explanation, he discovered that the only thing holding the pedal on was a single screw.[131] Burton R. Sims of Hempstead, Long Island, was equally unhappy with his '69 Lincoln Continental Mark III, for which he paid $9000. In his first fifteen thousand miles, the entire braking system had to be replaced seven times.[132]

One of the most blatant indications of the deterioration of modern cars is the bumper, which has become a frail mockery of what it used to be and

of what it is supposed to be. As many a rueful
motorist has discovered after surveying the damage
caused by a ten-miles-per-hour collision, the only
significant function served by today's bumpers is
decoration. Senator Nelson needled Automobile
Manufacturers Association president Thomas
Mann about this one day in Washington. Mann
claimed that "the automobile today is far safer
than it was a decade ago." Nelson replied, "We
had an interesting example of that about ten years
ago, where an old Model-T Ford ran into a new
Cadillac and the Ford went away without a dent
and there was about $700 worth of damage to the
Cadillac. Ford had steel in the fender that folded
up the Cadillac. But nobody was hurt."

"You are not really saying," said Mann, "that
the Model-T Ford is a safer car than a Cadillac
today, are you?"

Nelson answered: "All I said is that they ran
into each other and the Cadillac barely walked
away." [133]

Studies have indicated that bumpers are easily
damaged beyond repair in accident impacts of less
than five or ten miles per hour. In the words of
Edward Daniels, Claim Manager of the Detroit
Automobile Interinsurance Exchange, "Most accidents involve front end damage. A functional
bumper that could contain the very frequent five-
to-ten mile an hour impact would reduce auto
accident losses by 20 percent, a cool billion dollars."[134]

Unfortunately, the bumpers on today's cars are incapable of "containing" even a *three* mile-per-hour bump, to say nothing of five or ten! "We haven't looked at the bumper as a safety device because of the large forces involved," said a top Ford engineer in 1968. "Its job is largely to protect the lights of the car in parking maneuvers. We consider that our bumpers provide this protection in impacts up to two miles an hour." Nor is the state-of-the-art of bumper technology any more advanced at Ford's "competitors." The chief engineer at Pontiac made the comment in 1969 that "The corporation has had this rule that bumpers must withstand a two-mile-an-hour collision. A few years ago we made some tests and found that very few of the industry's cars could withstand this. So I decided we'd build a bumper that could stand it."

The utter uselessness of such phony improvements is demonstrated by the plight of such no-nonsense car owners as taxi companies and police departments, whose businesslike attitudes toward the more irrational features of the vehicles they operate stand in sharp contrast to the passive ambivalence of most drivers. Many fleet owners have taken the problem into their own hands and fitted their cars with large wooden planks or water filled bumpers developed by outside firms. The auto manufacturers have frankly admitted that bumpers are the responsibility of stylists rather than engineers and that there is, as *Automotive News* engineering editor Joseph Callahan was told by the product engineering vice president of Ford in 1969, "no chance of doing anything that would protect the car in a ten-mile-an-hour crash." [135]

The problem is not that the engineers are incompetent but that the stylists are the ones who make up the rules. The current style demands that the bumper not protrude from the body of the car in an unseemly way. The bulging bumper of the 1969 Pontiac, which makes the car look as if it were wearing tight pants, is evidently quite seemly. On most cars, however, the trend has been to "French" the bumper in, to tuck it into the body in an integrated fashion. Then, naturally, if the bumper is smashed, the headlights, grille, fenders, and hood get smashed along with it.

An equally irrational feature of the modern bumper is its nonstandard distance from the ground. If two cars run together and their bumpers match in height, it is a lucky coincidence—assuming that the combined speed of the two vehicles is less than the speed of a slow walk. Because the heights of bumpers vary according to stylists' whims, collisions often result in "override"—one bumper passing over the other and smashing into the body. General Motors in 1969 began a feeble effort to standardize bumper heights in all of its divisions (in some cases even the front and rear bumpers of the same car don't match), but other makers have not yet cooperated. Their reasons are fascinating. For example, Roy Haeusler, Chrysler

Corporation's chief engineer for automotive safety, once claimed that uniform bumper heights are impossible because heights are affected by such factors as the vehicle's posture at the time of impact, depending on whether it is stopping, accelerating, or standing still. Yet Haeusler also indicated agreement with the industry's argument that the bumper is intended to be effective in parking maneuvers up to two or three miles per hour! One wonders whether the amount of dipping or rising a car's nose does at a speed of two or three miles per hour can really be the reason Chrysler feels it is hopeless to standardize the heights of its bumpers.

The appalling compromises to which Detroit's engineers are subjected in their handling of bumpers—and apparently of just about everything else, too—are put into graphic perspective by the performance of an automobile bumper developed in 1969 *outside* the industry by Menasco Manufacturing Company of Burbank, California, a company better known for its production of aircraft landing gear than for any contributions to automotive technology. As described in the July 28, 1969, issue of *Product Engineering,* the new bumper consists of four telescoping shock isolators, or "liquid springs," mounted in a W-pattern between the car frame and a conventional bumper. The isolator elements dissipate the impact energy "by making use of the visco-elastic properties of certain newly developed silicone elastomers at extremely high temperatures. . . . As the isolator shortens under the impact load, the elastomeric material inside is simultaneously reduced in volume and forced through small orifices and passages."

The Menasco researchers must have laughed at the goals which had been set by the auto industry's handcuffed engineers. After all, they reasoned, highway accidents occur at 30 mph, not 2 mph. While the auto companies played with chrome-plated compromises between "style" and "parking maneuvers," therefore, Menasco put to work its knowledge of shock isolation systems for Minuteman missile sites and came up with a bumper which was demonstrably capable of surviving crashes at *ten times* the speeds GM and Ford had publicly branded impossible. A late-model Chevrolet, equipped with the new Menasco bumper, showed little damage (the bumper was virtually unscathed and the trunk lid showed one small dent) after being subjected to repeated rear-end crashes by cars traveling up to 30 mph. In straight-on crashes, bumpers were undamaged at 26 mph.[136]

What is true of bumpers is also true of other parts. American motorists pay more than $6 *billion* each year to repair accident damage, mostly because the parts which are damaged are inexcusably expensive to repair. Headlamp assemblies, for example, are constructed in such a manner that the only way to obtain a new part, even a small one, is to buy a whole new assembly. In order to obtain a $2 component, for instance, it is often necessary to buy the whole $30 assembly. Labor costs are driven up when a fancy grille-bumper combination that couldn't stand a collision with a robin requires fifty-seven bolts and the efforts of three men to install and align.[137]

It is hard not to be cynical about the reasons for such absurd design. After all, a crumpled fender on a new car reduces the car's value considerably, and may hasten the purchase of a new car. In any case, it hastens the purchase of new parts, such as fenders, bumpers, and lights, which are even more profitable than new cars (it would cost $15,000 to buy the parts of a 1969 Chevrolet Impala separately and then assemble them).[138]

The manufacturers' disregard for quality is as apparent in the assembly of their cars as in the design. In either case, the guiding principle is always "What can we do to maintain the highest possible level of production?" But whereas the effect of this principle on design is rather devious (many consumers have no quarrel with technological obsolescence), the effect on the assembly line is quite direct: if there is a conflict between an assembly schedule and the elimination of a minor defect, the minor defect is sometimes deliberately overlooked. After all, what difference does one more defect make when the car is already riddled? [139] Studies of auto industry quality control made public in 1969 by Michigan Sen. Philip Hart, chairman of the Antitrust and Monopoly Subcommittee, show that the average American car has from twenty-six to forty defects and deficiencies when it is sold.[140]

When the owner of a new car drives unsuspectingly away in a vehicle containing twenty-six to forty defects and deficiencies, the results vary widely from case to case. Many buyers do not discover crucial problems until too late; the oil has leaked out, rain has leaked in, and further damage has been done. In some cases there may be damage to flesh as well as to machinery: as Hart's committee found, 50 percent of all new cars contain at least one major safety defect.

What happened to James W. Roberts, Jr., who moved to Alexandria, Virginia, shortly after buying a new 1968 Ford in Fayetteville, North Carolina, is typical of what is happening to drivers everywhere—and with increasing frequency. Roberts had no problems with his new car for nearly a month. Then, one day the car wouldn't start. A mechanic told him the starter would have to be fixed, but that his engine also required "major adjustment." Roberts had the work done as recommended.

Less than a month later, Roberts was driving on U.S. route 95 near Washington, D.C. Suddenly the bearings in the rear end fell out. The car was towed to a garage, and Roberts spent a day without transportation.

After another month the head gasket failed. Roberts took his car to a Springfield, Virginia, dealer, who told him that there was "water in the oil, and oil in the water." An assistant service man-

ager drew him aside and warned him that if he
drove the car in its present condition it would
"really mess the engine up." So Roberts left his
car in Springfield, Virginia, and went without
transportation for three days.

Not long after that, Roberts noticed his brakes
going bad. He took the car in to the dealership
for the necessary work but was told that parts had
to be ordered from Richmond. After three weeks
the parts had still not arrived. Roberts asked his
boss for a three-day pass to take the car back to
North Carolina "to have it fixed once and for all
and end my walking and riding a bus to work while
making car payments."

By the time he got to Fayetteville, the brakes
were so bad that the drums had to be turned. The
car had now traveled a grand total of six thousand
miles. After waiting for the brake repair (plus several other adjustments suggested by the service
manager), Roberts paid his bill and headed north.

As it turned out, however, the Fayetteville dealer
was not quite through with Mr. Roberts. Just before he reached the city limits, the seals in his
transmission blew out. Back to the service center
he was towed. The seals were duly replaced, Roberts returned to the road, and the car broke down
halfway to Virginia.

As the weather turned cold in the late fall of
1968, James Roberts' troubles went from bad to
worse. His battery went dead repeatedly, was repeatedly revived by men who assured him nothing

was wrong except that "the post needed cleaning," and persistently went dead again. In February Roberts fell ill and went to the hospital. His pregnant wife was left alone with the car. Unfortunately, it wouldn't start for her either. On the first morning, a service station man gave it a jump start, charged his fee, and left her with the warning *not to turn it off,* because it wouldn't start again and if they had to come back it would cost her again. "Of course," recalled Roberts, "she couldn't leave it running twenty-four hours a day." So she, too, drove it back to the dealer and was told nothing was wrong with the battery except that "the post needed cleaning."

During the next few weeks Roberts recovered but his car did not. The engine began leaking, the brakes went bad again, and Roberts decided to make a phone call to Henry Ford, II. Unfortunately, Mr. Ford was out of town. However, he did manage to speak with a Mr. Schmidt. He explained to Mr. Schmidt that his car "had not been repaired right" and asked what he should do. Schmidt suggested that Roberts take his car back to the dealer. Instead, Roberts hung up and mailed his warranty card back to Ford, saying it was no good, and could they "take the car back so I could buy another one. . . ."

Months later, James Roberts was still waiting to hear from Henry Ford. Although he was now relying mainly on a rented car for transportation, he was still struggling to salvage some use from his own car, which he described as follows:

"At the present time, the brakes pull to the left so bad it's dangerous to drive on highways; the transmission almost jumps out when going up a hill. The engine still leaks, and only half runs. Where the doors meet the frame, rain and snow comes inside. Where the roof was put together is cracked. The radio only works when you hit the dash. Some things are loose under the hood. . . .

"I put the car up for sale on the basis that the buyer would just take over the payments. However, after people drive it they won't even talk about buying it, say it is no good. I can't give it away; I can't buy another one because I'm stuck with this one; and I can't get any kind of help."[141]

Ford's failure to acknowledge this customer epitomizes the manufacturers' real attitudes toward the public they allegedly serve.[142] There were signs in 1970 that these attitudes might be changing, but critics found the job of distinguishing between mere lip service and real changes in policy increasingly difficult in the last two years of the decade. Ford, who had assumed a blatantly public-be-damned attitude as recently as 1969, was suddenly telling newsmen in 1970 that *pollution* had become a major concern of his company. The other companies, of course, were saying the same thing. Yet there was no evidence of significant changes on the roads or in the air. Advertising continued in the same vein as before. The makers showed little awareness that the country's needs had already shifted. Much effort was devoted to trying to shift the blame for the troubles of the automobile to the oil companies (for making leaded gas), the government (for interfering), the dealers (for sloppy service), and even the consumers (for complaining). In 1970, the major change was that the air was filled with talk of reform—much of it generated by Detroit—but the automotive juggernaut continued to roll as if nothing had happened at all.

III—DEALERS

In a country which seems to have an insatiable appetite for new cars, the new-car dealer would seem to have an enviable job. On one hand, he has the advantages of independence (the business is his). On the other hand, he is backed by the marketing power of a giant manufacturing corporation. Advertisements for his product are carried by every major newspaper, magazine, and television channel, and these products are known to every potential customer. He can guarantee his product without hesitation, because the manufacturer stands ready to pay the full cost of repair. He has no worries about customer financing, because the organization takes care of that, too. He is one of the shrewdest, most aggressive of all types of businessmen, and he has his hands on one of the richest markets in the world.

It seems incredible, therefore, that the independent auto dealer is a fast-diminishing breed. On January 1, 1949, there were fifty thousand dealerships in the United States. By January 1, 1969, that number had dropped to twenty-seven thousand, a decrease of more than a thousand dealers per year for twenty consecutive years.[143] The reasons for this decline have been obscured by bitter controversy, but there is evidence that the principal threat to the dealer is the very thing which threatens the customers and the environment at large—the burgeoning power of the manufacturers.

Dealers are often regarded by consumers as the representatives and disciples of Detroit, the proselytizers of the car culture. Actually, the dealers are the hypotenuse in a sticky triangle involving both the manufacturers and their customers. If dealers are aggressive, it is partly because they are constantly taking it on the nose from both the manufacturers (whose financial power casts an ever longer shadow over the dealers' independence) and the customers (who blame dealers for all the troubles they have with cars).

Customers have plenty to be unhappy about. When makers spend more money on lifting the faces of cars than on improving the reliability of engines and wheels, it is inevitable that cars will be plagued with trouble. Yet it is often the dealer who is blamed, since it is he who assured the customer that the car was a good buy, and who took his money. It is also the dealer who gets the business when the car repeatedly breaks down.

In the "after" business—the vast volume of service, repair, and replacement work necessary to keep cars on the road after they have been purchased—the dealers are not entirely blameless for customers' woes. This is particularly true for the business which takes place after the new-car warranty period is up, since the makers are no longer scrutinizing the books for overcharges. Dealers, however, get less and less of the after-business as a car gets older. Work then shifts to repair shops which do not deal in new or used cars.[144] Responsibility for a car's failures become increasingly those of careless owners, repairmen, and the forces of natural deterioration.

The area in which the dealers are most heavily condemned is in the selling of a new car, an area in which the makers' influence is particularly evident. It is too easy to assume that what happens in the showroom is out of the makers' hands. Whereas blame for a faulty machine can only be laid on the factory, it might seem, a sneaky selling job is purely the responsibility of the dealer. In 1969, however, California Deputy District Attorney Charles O'Brien disagreed strongly with this view. What happens in the salesroom, he said, is a direct function of what happens around the gleaming board room tables of Detroit.

The part of the process which is visible to the public begins, O'Brien told the Federal Trade Commission, when the dealer places a newspaper ad containing such statements as $1204 OFF LIST" and "FACTORY LIST PRICE $4489, HERE $3689." The customer goes to the lot, where he is greeted by a gregarious young man who offers to assist him in selecting and purchasing an automobile.

"Harry Carbuyer believes that this pleasant individual is a salesman. This is not a salesman," said O'Brien. "It is a greeter. His first job is to determine if Harry is a tire-kicker or a serious customer.

"If Harry asks to see the 'leaders,' the cars that were advertised at such fabulous savings, he will be ushered to the back row of the lot. The fabulous buys are not the shiny cars in the showroom, because they haven't been washed. The color selection is limited to black. Much of the chrome seems to be missing. And, they don't have all of the desirable equipment—such as automatic transmissions.

"Well, that wasn't quite what Harry had in mind. He'd like to see some other cars. Harry sees one he'd like, and he asks, 'How much?' The greeter-salesman looks at the window price-sticker and announces the bottom-line price. The game begins. Harry says 'How much off?' The greeter says, 'Well, Mr. Carbuyer, how much do you think you want to pay?' Harry says, 'I don't know, as little as possible!' The greeter begins to work downward in steps of $100.

"Let's assume that the sticker price is $4,200. The greeter says, 'How about $4,100?' Harry says, 'Too much!' '$4,000?' 'Hell, no! This is supposed to be an economy car.' And the game continues until the greeter determines whether Harry is really serious or just shopping. If it turns out that Harry is serious but wants the $4,200 car for $3,000, the greeter says, 'Come on in the office and we'll see what we can do.'

"Now, Harry thinks he can get this automobile

for $3,000. He signs a purchase order, makes a deposit and gives the greeter the keys to the old clunker which he is trading in. He signs a credit application and fills out forms to transfer ownership of the trade-in to the dealer. Then the salesman says, 'I'll have to get this approved.'

"Harry never sees the friendly greeter again.

"Now the real salesman appears, bearing an impressive title: 'Sales Manager' or 'Credit Manager'. In the trade, he's called a 'closer'.

"The closer tells Harry that it's impossible to sell this car, this acme of the automotive art, for $3,000. The greeter made a mistake . . . the factory won't permit a sale at this price . . . in fact, it is an illegal sale-below-cost. That's what the closer says.

"The closer spends a couple of hours with Harry. He figures and re-figures the price. Harry is drained by the experience. Ultimately, the $4,200 car which he was buying for $3,000 will cost him $3,700. Harry does not protest. During the two hours the closer has convinced Harry that he is still getting a good deal—$500 under sticker price. A bargain. Not a maxi-bargain, but still more than a mini-bargain.

"Harry sees himself in the saddle, master of this machine. He hesitates. Reality begins to force itself in upon his dream.

"The closer has an answer. Harry's deposit is locked in a safe; the girl with the combination has gone home. His old car has been sent to another his wife and discuss the purchase. He offers Harry a phone, and politely leaves the room to provide Harry with privacy.

"Then the closer goes around the corner and picks up the extension so he can listen to Harry's conversation and determine his attitude. If Harry brings his wife along, the closer listens to their private conversation on eaves-dropping equipment installed in the agency.

"One dealer actually attempted to refute our charges on sales activities by supplying us with tape recordings of customers' conversations.

"This, briefly, is what faces the car buyer."[145]

Apparently, such activities aren't confined to California. Similar shenanigans were reported by Washington *Evening Star* columnist Philip Love. After getting three different "list" prices (and three different trade-in prices) for the same new model from three dealers, Love and his wife chose one for which the trade-in was $1,075.45, and were ushered into the salesman's office. The salesman then filled out an order blank. Love recalled that "after he'd filled out the order blank, but before my wife gave him the required deposit, he suddenly excused himself and left the office. There were two books on his desk, and she picked up one and idly thumbed through it. To her amazement, the car we were buying for $2,961.75 was listed at $2,887!

" 'You seem to have made a mistake,' she told the salesman when he returned a few minutes later. 'The price listed here is $74.75 less than the one

you gave me.' He looked, blinked, gulped and ex-
claimed: 'Oh, I *have* made a mistake. I'll have to
straighten it out with my boss. Excuse me.' He was
back in a few minutes with the lower price initialed
by his boss and those mysterious forty-five cents
gone from the trade-in allowance. 'I don't know
how I made such a mistake,' he said. 'I must have
been confused.' "[146]

It is no wonder that dealers have been stung by
public outrage. It seems incredible that anything
Detroit might do could justify such penny-arcade
practices. Of course, such practices may be exceptional, although O'Brien implied that they were
typical. But O'Brien also made it clear that he
believes these practices are fostered by Detroit, not
by the dealers themselves. They begin when the
manufacturer advertises a "list" price which the
buyer assumes to be the "normal" selling price of
the car. Actually, the list price is a fiction invented
by the makers—a price far higher than that for
which the dealer can sell the car and still make
a profit.[147] The discrepancy tempts most dealers to
offer enormous "discounts." Other dealers must
then offer large discounts also, in order to remain
competitive. The actual selling price drops far
below list everywhere, so that the discounts are
in effect not discounts but normal prices. The result
is that the customer thinks he has a big bargain,
when actually he is paying the same as everyone
else. This bit of deception stimulates the market—a
situation which is more advantageous to the manu-

facturers than to the dealers, since manufacturers make their profit from market penetration while dealers are more dependent on profit margin. Meanwhile, the near-universality of discounting produces a bartering atmosphere, which is confusing enough in a country where consumers are accustomed to fixed prices. But the meaning of prices is further confused by the makers' proliferation of models and options which generate so many additions, subtractions, and qualifications that even the dealers are sometimes mixed up about what is "standard" and what is "extra." As a Ford official boasted in 1969, "We can run our assembly plants at maximum capacity, maximum overtime 365 days a year and not build the same car twice." [148]

This is only the beginning of the manufacturers' influence on dealer practices. The problem is that dealers are highly independent businessmen who do not like to be cast as cogs in a giant corporate wheel. Many are anxious to prove that if dealer practices are infuriating to customers, it is only because the manufacturers have forced the dealers into such practices by creating an impossible marketing situation at the retail level. Ed Mullane, a Bergenfield, New Jersey, Ford dealer who viewed the worsening reputation of the auto dealers in the 1950s and 1960s with growing discomfort, spent most of 1969 traveling around the country speaking to dealers, warning them of the dangers of what he called "factory tyranny," and the things he had to say struck a responsive chord wherever he went.

The distinction between the "two worlds" of automobile marketing (wholesale and retail) became a heated issue among dealers who felt they were being victimized by the manufacturers' growing disregard for some of the fundamental principles of free enterprise. By early 1968 the issue had reached, at least for a substantial number of new-car dealers, crisis proportions, and by the end of the following year, Ford and Chrysler dealers in urban and suburban areas were on the brink of open rebellion against Detroit.

The grumbling began with a series of scattered events which drew little attention from the press but which were viewed with alarm by thousands of automobile dealers across the country. In Allegheny County, Pennsylvania, a new Dodge agency opened with the usual hoopla. Shortly afterward, several other hitherto successful Dodge agencies in the county began to fail. In New York City, a new Ford dealership opened. Again, other Ford dealerships in the area began to fail. In Morris County, New Jersey, plans were announced for a new Dodge service center. Shortly afterward, the Chrysler Corporation announced that a Dodge dealership which had done a successful business in that county for many years was about to go out of business.

These events might easily have been chalked off as the normal casualties of a competitive system.

Mullane and a number of other dealers claimed otherwise. There were many more failing dealerships than new ones, they said, and there was a very interesting difference between the "failures" and the newcomers. Each of the failures was a privately financed business managed by a man who had invested everything he was worth in the operation—and who knew just how much he could cut his prices and still make a profit. Each of the newcomers, by contrast, was a freewheeling operation that succeeded only by cutting prices with reckless abandon and cutting them so low that no private dealer, no matter how efficient his management, could possibly match them without going broke. The explanation, said Mullane, was that the new outfits were operating deep in the red, and the reason they could afford to do so was that they were being subsidized by the manufacturers.

The first reaction of the dealers was a mixture of anger and bewilderment. Why in the world would a manufacturing company want to compete with its own franchised dealers? Certainly the answer was not to improve the franchisees' performance by keeping them on their toes! The effect of the subsidized stores, or "factory" stores, as they came to be known, was to drive the independents out of business, not to stimulate them to new heights of performance. And to top it off, a number of dealers found that they were being undersold in the used car market as well as the new—by leasing companies and other fleet owners (such as government agencies), which could afford to dispose of used rental cars at under-market prices because they were getting their new cars from factories at lower prices than those paid by the dealers.

As the number of factory-financed outlets increased, the strategy of the manufacturers became clear. The Big Three have always measured their performance in terms of how big a slice of the sales pie they have, and there is nothing Ford and Chrysler enjoy more than stealing a percentage point from one another, unless it is stealing a point or two from GM! One of the easiest ways to increase market penetration is to sell at a loss. The trick, of course, is that the loss at the retail level is not as great as the resulting profit at the wholesale level. With most of the manufacturer's overhead met by a given volume of sales, the manufacturer's profit on all "extra" units is substantially larger than the average profit of the preceding units, large enough to subsidize the factory store's operating losses and still leave a profit for the manufacturer. The one company which might have good reason *not* to increase its share of the market is, naturally, General Motors, which with more than half of the world's largest sales pie already under its belt, finds itself sitting under the baleful eye of the Justice Department's antitrust division. Significantly, GM dealers have not had to contend with very many factory stores. (One authority on automobile law believes, however, that GM is simply biding its time until Ford and Chrysler have become well enough

established for GM to be able to begin full-scale
retail operations with the excuse that it is merely
responding to the competitive advantage gained by
its rivals.)

Claims that the manufacturers intend to "take
over" the retail industry (gradually replacing independent franchises with factory-owned and
controlled outlets) are laughed off by the manufacturers, who say the whole issue has been "blown
out of perspective." In answer to a query, Thomas
Mann, president of the Automobile Manufacturers
Association, claimed in 1969 that when a dealer
goes out of business the reason lies not in the competition from manufacturers' outlets, but in "the
trend towards larger, more efficient business outlets
throughout our economy (e.g., the small corner
grocery store is gradually being replaced by larger
food stores, the small farms are gradually being
replaced by larger ones, etc.)," as well as in "a trend
of some years and in many businesses to move away
from high rent areas in the central business districts
toward the suburbs." [149]

Mann's observations appear to be consistent with
the facts (to the extent that the facts are known)
about the locations of factory stores. The area
which has apparently been hardest hit by factory
competition is the New York metropolitan area,
particularly Manhattan. "The tragedy of the automobile marketplace is nowhere more apparent
than in my own city of New York," testified Representative Benjamin S. Rosenthal in hearings on

auto prices held by the Federal Trade Commission in 1969. "On Manhattan Island it is impossible to buy a Chevrolet or a Cadillac or a Ford or a Mercuty or a Lincoln from an independent auto dealer. Every sales outlet for these cars is owned by the manufacturer. Thus, the manufacturer effectively controls distribution and thereby the price in the prime American auto market. This practice of manufacturers owning sales outlets—instead of selling through independent dealers—is spreading throughout the metropolitan New York area and is already apparent elsewhere in the country." [150] In fact, the Senate Monopoly Subcommittee claims to have evidence that on a percentage basis there are even more—albeit less publicized—factory stores in the rest of the country than there are in New York City.[151]

The irony of Rosenthal's testimony is that while it confirms the dealers' fears of a noncompetitive market, it also points to a danger quite different from that anticipated by the dealers. The dealers, of course, are concerned about being squeezed out by prices that are too low. Rosenthal is concerned about car buyers being squeezed by prices that are too *high*. Yet the two concerns are not contradictory; the double-edged danger of the factory store idea is that *after* competition has been destroyed by low prices at the retail level, it would be possible for the prices to rise with nothing but the good will of the manufacturers and the porous shield of government regulation to stop them. Such a prospect assumes, of course, that the only real competition in auto prices is at the retail level. This, precisely, is what many dealers, as well as many economists and other industry-watchers, now believe to be the case.

What confuses the issue of competition is the fact that the industry is often judged in terms of its most conspicuous and available members—the automobile dealers, but the market for dealers is quite different from the market for manufacturers, and it would be a ludicrous mistake to confuse the two. As Raphael Cohen, chairman of the Metropolitan Independent Dodge-Chrysler Dealer Association, told the Federal Trade Commission in 1969, "One of the grave errors that is made when discussing whether there is, or is not, competition in the auto industry is brought about by the manner in which the question is posed. I believe the question should be stated in the following fashion: Is there *meaningful* competition in the auto industry that takes place to benefit the consumer, who is the largest segment of the society? The reason that I make this distinction is not to split hairs, but to really arrive at the crux of the problem.

"One need only open any newspaper or magazine, turn on any radio or television station, and he can find one of four manufacturers fiercely competing for his business. Examine the same newspaper and the dealer is offering all kinds of goodies to the purchaser for the opportunity of selling him a car. So, to flatly state that competition does not take place, brings me to defend a position that can be easily refuted."

However, the competition among manufacturers, said Cohen, has no effect on the wholesale prices of their products. "In an asymmetrical oligopoly the leader, in this case General Motors, sets the price standards for the industry and the others merely comply. The only place that meaningful competition exists is on the retail level." [152] In the car-price hearings, Rosenthal stated: "We all recognize that the American consumer needs help to protect his rights and interests in the general marketplace. But in the automobile segment of that marketplace, the consumer has *no* rights. The terms and conditions under which the average American purchases an automobile are dictated to him in a marketplace clouded by monopoly and dulled by a lack of meaningful competition."

Neither Rosenthal nor Cohen (nor anyone else outside Detroit) claimed to know how many factory-financed stores there are, but both were convinced that the number is large—and growing. The makers said it isn't so. John B. Naughton, general manager of Ford division, rejected not only the whole theory that the competitive system is being jeopardized, but the facts on which the theory is based. Ford, he said, had almost six thousand dealerships of which only thirteen were wholly owned company stores. While freely admitting that these stores tend to undersell the independent dealers, Naughton claimed he personally "abhorred" com-

pany stores and that "all the people here are dedi-
cated to eliminating them. . . . In 1967, when I
became assistant general manager, we had
twenty-nine stores. Only five of those twenty-nine
are still factory-owned. Twenty-four of those stores
have been disposed of, while eight others have been
added." The only reason Ford Division is in the
retail business at all, he asserted, is to protect its
market when an independent dealer goes out of
business and no other independent dealer is willing
to replace him at the same location. He said that
Ford then takes over the operation of the store
itself with the intention of selling it to an independent dealer as soon as one can be found.[153]

Unfortunately, Naughton's assurances pertain
only to *wholly owned* company stores, which account for only a small percentage of the company
financing with which dealers are concerned. In
addition to those outlets which are owned outright
by the manufacturers, there are hundreds and perhaps thousands more in which the manufacturers
maintain a partial financial interest. According to
the dealers, this interest is in many cases large
enough to give the manufacturer complete control
of the operation. In a statement before the Senate
Small Business Monopoly Subcommittee in July
1969, Alexander Hammond, a New York attorney
who has represented a number of dealers in cases
involving franchise failures, described how this
control works:

"Companies are erecting large numbers of elaborate and costly facilities without reasonable expectation that these real estate investments will return a fair profit. In the last few years Chrysler has built over six hundred large dealership facilities for lease to controlled and nominally uncontrolled dealers, and new facilities are constantly being erected.[154] Dealers whose existence naturally depends upon the renewal of the leases for their facilities and upon the amount of rent they must pay are obviously subject to continuing domination and control." [155]

While Naughton's Ford Division has only thirteen company stores, it is involved in 177 dealer development stores—stores which are owned partly by the maker and partly by the dealer. Curiously, Ford refuses to disclose the percentages of its interests in these dealerships. Thus, the number of dealerships legally controlled by Ford Division is a *minimum* of thirteen but *could* be anywhere from thirteen to 190! (In the Chrysler system, the maker maintains total control of any store in which it holds an interest, no matter how small.) Furthermore, it is not clear that Ford does *not* control any store which is not wholly or partially owned by Ford. Other methods of control may be possible, and Hammond claimed that by 1969 such methods had become widespread. Many dealerships which appear to be independent businesses are actually controlled by the manufacturers, he said. "They hide this by a hundred and one devious mechanisms . . . but the proof of control is the fact that *all the money flows in one direction."* [156]

Furthermore, while Naughton would evidently have it appear that a factory store (or dealer development store) opens only when an independent business has failed in spite of itself and no other remedy is available, this is at best a half-truth. The other half is illustrated by the case of Schwartz Dodge, a thirty-five-year-old family-run dealership in Dover, New Jersey. The facts in the Schwartz case are quite simple and are distinguished from other, similar cases only by the fact that the manufacturer's takeover was foiled—temporarily, at least—by a judge's writ. In order to fulfill the terms of his contract with a manufacturer, a franchised dealer is ostensibly required to meet a "minimum sales requirement" set by the manufacturer, based on the amount of territory assigned to the dealership. In January 1966, Schwartz's territory was "modified" by the Chrysler Corporation. Whereas it had previously included only the immediate area around Dover (a town of twenty thousand), it now suddenly included the entire Newark metropolitan area (a 70 by 40-mile stretch encompassing several million people). Schwartz's minimum sales requirement was increased accordingly, and, not surprisingly, he failed to meet it. Chrysler then issued a notice of termination. After thirty-seven years of success in the business, Herb Schwartz and his family were about to have their franchise pulled out from under them, even though, as was later established, the growth in sales of Schwartz Motors had exceeded Dodge's nationwide growth percentage for the previous five years. The whole thing seemed incomprehensible—until it was established that Chrysler had made plans (had in fact applied for a variance on a property) to build a factory store in nearby Mountain Lakes.[157]

On the grounds that Schwartz was being asked to fulfill a sales quota "considerably higher than other comparable Dodge dealers," Federal District Judge Joseph Collihan granted a restraining order against Dodge Division permitting Schwartz to continue operating while the judge mulled over the results of two days of pretrial hearings. The testimony was highly revealing, not only because it provided a classic illustration of the kind of intimidation to which dealers claim they are being subjected with increasing frequency, but also because it blatantly contradicted the manufacturers' contention that factory stores are established only as a last resort to protect a territory which a failing independent has abandoned. The evidence seemed to support the dealer's belief that Chrysler was trying to *make* him fail, and that if he wouldn't stumble on his own sufficiently to meet the established criterion for failure, Chrysler would adjust its criterion for failure accordingly.

Perhaps the most significant aspect of the case was delineated by Judge Collihan, who subsequently issued an injunction to permit Schwartz to continue selling Dodge cars pending a jury trial. The judge wrote: "It is clear that, given the method by which minimum sales requirement is calculated, approximately one half of all Chrysler dealers would be subject to termination at any time by virtue of the Minimum Sales Requirement clause." [158] Observers of the Schwartz case were wondering whether perhaps that was what Chrysler Corporation had in mind all along.

The Schwartz case was by no means unique. Termination—or, as some dealers tended to think of it, extermination—became, in the decade between 1960 and 1970, a source of palpable fear in the automobile retail business. Herb Schwartz was not the only dealer to take to the courts to save his life's work. The week before news of the Schwartz injunction broke, Walter C. Jennings, a Chrysler-Plymouth dealer in Little Rock, Arkansas, filed suit against Chrysler Corporation, charging that his franchise had been canceled as a result of a two-year conspiracy by Chrysler in violation of the Sherman Antitrust Act.[159] The circumstances of the Jennings cancellation were almost identical with those of the Schwartz cancellation.

All this prompted Mullane to claim that dealers were turning into "the lackeys of the manufacturers." In October 1969, he told an interviewer, "The manufacturers beat the dealers into submission. . . . We fought two wars to be independent, and what do we have? *Feudalism.* Witchcraft and sorcery in the fourteenth century had nothing on what Detroit pulls on us. . . ." [160] The following month he called for a "Magna Charta" to set dealers free from "arbitrary and tyrannical factory rule." Looking and sounding more like a poet than a car dealer, the angry, white-haired Mullane told a group of New Jersey dealers that modern factory-dealer relations were comparable to conditions existing in England prior to the issuance of the Magna Charta in the thirteenth century. "Like the barons of King John, the dealer body will no longer sit by and futilely petition for help," he said. He then presented a detailed plan for the total elimination of factory-subsidized competition and factory interference with independent businesses, concluding that the only hope for insuring "corporate responsibility" in the auto manufacturing industry was to form a new dealer-consumer coalition to pressure Congress and the courts for mutual protection in the form of both passage of new legislation and enforcement of old laws which have been conveniently disregarded for years.[161]

Mullane was not alone in his assessment. Lyman Slack, president of the National Automobile Dealers Association, pointed out in 1969 that the "factory store" was only one of several abuses of the franchise system being used to enrich the makers at the expense of the dealers.[162] One of the main sources of a dealer's income was the sale of accessories for new cars, such as the radios sold by Automatic Radio Company. There had been a time—in the 1940s and 1950s—when dealers stocked accessories manufactured by a variety of companies. If a customer wanted accessories for his new car, the dealer happily provided them, taking both a profit for the part and a fee for its installation. In the 1960s, however, the car makers had begun to muscle in on the action. The technique was simple: if a customer wanted an air conditioner, the auto manufacturer installed his own brand of air conditioner at the factory, taking the profit and installation fee for himself. The dealer (along with the independent air conditioner manufacturer) was excluded from the transaction entirely, and the customer had no choice of brands.

Between 1964 and 1968, the percentage of radios installed at the factory (rather than at the dealership) had increased from 64 percent to 88 percent, while air conditioners had risen from 17 percent to 43 percent.[163]

This method of short-circuiting the sales of accessories was not entirely new, but it was treated with far more indulgence by the government than similar practices had been treated in the past. In 1942, the Federal Trade Commission issued a "cease and desist" order against General Motors, which it found had "adopted a program of acts and practices which were designed to and did intimidate and coerce its dealers and compel them to purchase parts and accessories solely from the selling corporation, and prohibited purchases from outside sources, except in cases of emergency. The result of this type of acts and practices was that independent jobbers, selling the products of independent manufacturers, were unable to sell to dealers such parts and accessories as heaters, radios, antifreeze solutions, spark plugs, etc.; the dealers of the General Motors Sales Corporation were intimidated, coerced and compelled to purchase accessories and auto parts only through it." [164]

In this connection, it is interesting to note that a document from Ford Motor Company, which found its way into the possession of Ralph Nader, shows that in 1966 Ford made far higher markups over the costs of its cars and parts than it allowed its dealers to charge.[165] These findings were further corroborated by Robert W. Crandall, assistant professor of economics at the Massachusetts Institute of Technology, who testified in 1969 that the ever-increasing vertical integration of the auto manufacturing companies enables the makers to control more and more of the total sales of parts. Dealers, he said, are pressured to use "authorized" parts instead of those which may be available from independent companies. He cited figures to show that independent garages use fewer "authorized" parts than dealers—and have lower prices.[166]

Profit opportunities for dealers are further reduced by the makers' taboo against "multiple" dealerships. Less than 3 percent of all domestic dealerships are intercorporate duals—showrooms where customers can compare cars of two different manufacturers. One apparent reason for this absurd taboo is that it heightens the barrier to new competition. "I wonder how many household appliances would have gotten into the marketplace if the manufacturer of that appliance had to set up stores all over the country," asked Nader in 1968.[167] Single-company retail outlets are to the advantage of the makers, but not necessarily to the dealers. The almost complete absence of multiples is further evidence that the franchise system is a tool of Detroit more than a reciprocal arrangement between two segments of the economy.

Even in areas where competition from factory stores is not an immediate problem, therefore, its shadow lurks over the system; for when a dealer has been sufficiently sapped by the encroachment of the manufacturer *within* his operation, he may capitulate anyway. When he finally "cops out" of the business because it has not been profitable, he is unlikely to find a successor eager to make the rather substantial investment required to start a business. Naturally, the franchise will fall into the hands of the manufacturer, whose only alternatives are to open a factory store, or to find an "operator" who is willing to manage the business under the manufacturer's direction, and with the manufacturer's financial backing. It matters little whether the factory takeover is deliberate or not, since the effect on the market is the same. "Once this process has taken hold, it generates its own increased momentum, which may not easily be controlled by the manufacturer," warned Alexander Hammond. "A manufacturer will seek to explain or defend the establishment of a new factory dealership in some location as being necessary for it to retain its normal percent of penetration in that market. The explanation appears creditable until the economic forces which created the necessity for such action are examined: it is the manufacturer's own retail practices and sometimes those of its overzealous competitors which have financed dealerships out of business. Once economic forces are put in motion, they do not depend on the intention or good will of men, and they are inexorable and often irreversible."

Nor were the forces always purely economic. In the late 1960s, hundreds of franchisees complained of coercion. A Missouri dealer with a forty-five-day inventory of new cars received seventeen phone calls from the manufacturer in one day, beginning at the local level and ending with Detroit sales brass, all insisting that he buy more. Another Missouri dealer had a sales quota of ten cars a month but could get deliveries of only three or four a month from the factory; yet, he was cautioned that his franchise would be canceled if his quotas were not met. A New York dealer repeatedly received shipments of new cars equipped with expensive options he had never ordered, and the manufacturer insisted that he pay for them. A Pontiac, Michigan, dealer, who made a speech complaining that the manufacturer deprived him of potential customers by giving cars to Pontiac executives at a discount, had his franchise canceled for "disloyalty." [168] A New York dealer was required, in a bizarre inversion of the normal competitive situation, to submit monthly financial statements to his franchisor, who also happened to be operating a nearby company store. "By contract," said the dealer, "I am forced to supply my competition with my operating statement. I believe that this is the most ridiculous thing I have ever heard." None of these situations were unusual; most were repeated hundreds of times and in every part of the country.

In their direct dealings with the manufacturers, what upset the dealers as much as anything else was the warranty system for new car repairs. Hundreds of dealers claimed they were losing money on warranty work—work they were required to do whether they could make a living at it or not. A 1968 study conducted for the National Auto Dealers Association by Management Information Corporation of Chicago showed that dealers were making $2.45 less per warranty job than they were for similar nonwarranty work. This study was based on data from twenty thousand repair orders in four hundred dealerships. It was later corroborated by a study of twenty-nine Ford and Lincoln-Mercury dealerships (conducted for Ford by Arthur Anderson & Company).[169] Dealers contended that factories were making elaborate promises to customers in their warranties, insisting that the dealers fulfill these promises, then failing to fork over enough reimbursement to cover the cost of doing so. For the dealers, the only solution was to raise the prices of nonwarranty work. As a result, dealers were taking the blame for everything that was wrong both with warranty workmanship and with non-warranty prices. A substantial number of dealers felt that being simultaneously squeezed by Detroit and maligned by the rest of the country was more than they could stand. The business, they said, had become brutal and impersonal. While some were being driven out of business or canceled by the makers, others decided to quit the business without waiting for disaster. There were some who said they thought the entire franchise system was doomed.

Resignation, however, was not the prevailing mood. Many dealers, refusing to concede that their only reason for existence was to contribute—by sacrificing themselves, if necessary—to the juggernaut in Detroit, appealed to fellow dealers for help. In the New York-New Jersey metropolitan area, Ford dealers who felt that their dealer organization was being used against them by Ford Motor Company formed a new regional "Ford Dealers Alliance," with no ties to the manufacturer.

The Alliance idea began to germinate in the first months of 1969, when the inadequacies of both the manufacturers' "dealer councils" and the supposedly independent National Automobile Dealers Association became painfully clear to dealers in the New York area who, according to *Automotive News* editor Robert M. Finlay, wanted to "elevate the status of the metropolitan auto dealer to that of a sound businessman who will win a reputation for ethical dealing." At the NADA conference in February, there was talk of forming a new national association, tentatively called the National Federation of Metro Market Dealers, not as a rival to NADA but as a supplementary organization which would devote its full resources to solving the problems of dealers in metropolitan markets, including the problem of what Finlay called "overproduction by the auto makers and sales and practices and advertising by big-city wheelers who move the excess production by volume practices other dealers consider harmful to the public, the trade, and the reputation of all dealers." [170]

The leader of the movement, however, was not even present at the conference. Ed Mullane, the Bergenfield, New Jersey, Ford dealer, who had been a member of the national Ford Dealer Council a year earlier and who had been elected to a second term as a regional delegate by the Newark Council, was banned from the national conference when an obscure rule was invoked by Ford—a rule which prohibited any national Council member from serving again, even as a regional representative, until two years had elapsed. The rule had never been enforced before; yet Ford refused to accept the Newark Council's request that Mullane (who had criticized the company severely for its involvement with company stores) be recognized as its elected representative. When Ford officials set up a meeting to elect someone else, the dealers defied the company by reelecting Mullane, and when Ford subsequently refused to seat Mullane at a meeting of the Northeastern Regional Ford Dealers Council, the Newark and New York representatives stood up and walked out. In later conversation, one dealer asked: "If they are sincere in their dealings with us, why make an issue of Mullane? Maybe they fear he's getting close to their jugular?" Another declared: "I have just staked my entire fortune on Ford Motor Company by putting all my money in a new, larger facility. Why can't Ford Division have the same faith in me and other dealers by letting the Dealer Council really be the voice of the dealers, and not an instrument of the company, which in this case was used to further a personal vendetta?"

Within three months of its formation, the Alliance had made its first big move. In August 1969, seeking to bar factory retailing and other interference with business transactions between dealers and their customers, the Alliance filed a suit against Ford Motor Company in the Superior Court of New Jersey. It was the first time in history that franchised auto dealers had moved en masse against their franchisor in the courts. Several months later, a new "Chevrolet Dealers Alliance" was formed in Arkansas, a sign that GM had begun to flex its muscles as had been feared.[171]

When wind of the growing struggle reached Washington, both Congress and the Federal Trade Commission held hearings to assess possible needs for federal regulation. It was quickly discovered that automobile dealers on the whole felt deep ambivalence about such regulation. While a number of specific grievances were discussed, it became clear that the gut issue was the fact that one group of independent businessmen felt itself being squashed, economically and psychologically, under the thumb of another. The dealers, much as they hated their submissive roles, were wary of the government simply becoming another thumb. Even so, by 1970 there were many, including the leadership of NADA, who were willing to cry Uncle Sam. Apparently not everyone in Washington had sold out to Detroit, and the prospects of getting legislative relief seemed good. The Senate Small Business Committee was interested, and so was the Antitrust and Monopoly Subcommittee. The Federal Trade Commission, stung by accusations of incompetence and complacency, pursued a sharp investigation of deceptive pricing.

As testimony accumulated in courts and legislative hearings, it became increasingly clear that the crisis in manufacturer-dealer relations had become significant, not only for the dealer and the franchise system of automotive marketing, but for the future of small businesses everywhere—and, by implication, for the future of free enterprise itself. In the Small Business hearings held in July 1969, Alexander Hammond said that "automotive retailing is a large business affecting the fortunes and lives of hundreds of thousands of people employed in the business. The increased takeover of the retailing business by automobile manufacturers will disastrously affect and eventually destroy great

numbers of manufacturers and suppliers of accessories, parts and supplies who presently are able
to compete with automobile manufacturers in supplying some of these products to independent
dealers." The failure of government to reverse this
trend could create dangerous precedents—and
temptations—for other industries. The effect on
people who buy cars would be sad to behold. With
the last stronghold of genuine competition in the
automobile industry gone (much is gone already),
the process of buying a car might be more like
paying an income tax than shopping in a marketplace. Prices would be high and bargaining useless.
The customer would take what he was offered by
the consolidated industry—or leave it. But he really
wouldn't even have that choice, since cars are, as
everyone knows, the only way of "getting there."
Of course, for the sake of keeping public nerves
well tranquilized, the game of competition would
probably be continued in a more innocuous form.
As Representative Rosenthal observed, "Once in
control of all sales outlets, General Motors or Ford
will be able to create an illusion of competition
by offering trading stamps, prizes, etc. . . ."

Though dealers for the most part must go along,
willingly or unwillingly, with Detroit's policies, the
makers are not taking their minions' loyalty entirely for granted. Several kinds of attempts have
been made to keep dealers' interests separate from
those of the public. Retailers and consumers *do*
have different perspectives, and these have been

cleverly exploited. Thus, dealers are distressed about prices too low and customers about prices too high, and although both concerns arise from different stages of the same disease, they are made to appear contradictory. Manufacturers have also attempted to divide their opposition by suggesting that antipollution campaigns may be rough on dealers and by invoking an already instinctive fear of government regulation and consumer revolution.

Intimidation from Detroit, combined with the threat of radical changes in automotive technology and consumer demands, only intensifies the natural insecurity of auto dealers. Already in a state of near-crisis, retailers are likely to be torn deeply. Some, perhaps many, are bound to be loyal to the hand that supplies them. A dealer named James V. Mancusco, for example, is repelled by what he calls the "era of the complainer." As he sees it, there is a silent majority of dealers who, like the silent majority of Americans in general, are quite happy with their lot. Mancusco apparently feels it is splitting hairs to distinguish between dealers and manufacturers; to him they are all "the auto industry."[172]

Others show an independence which is far more pronounced than that of most big-corporation people. Most of these dealers are intensely proud of their businesses and are loathe to be regarded as villains by the public. Their concern about the public image of their profession, along with a growing sense of responsibility for the social impacts of cars, may help to tip the scales against Detroit; for dealers do not want to add to the stigma of dishonesty that of social and environmental irresponsibility. Particularly revealing in this connection is a letter written by a GM dealer who has watched the evolution of the American automobile, year by year, since its earliest days. Responding to GM president Cole's claims that critics' charges are "unrealistic" and "ridiculous," the dealer (who asked that his name be withheld) wrote in a July 1969 letter to *Automotive News:*

"... Now, Mr. Cole, are they? When GM delivers cars to its dealers that have so many things wrong with them that it takes three to four times more time to precondition them for delivery to the customer . . .? Just what would you call this? When you cheapen the material in cars, what does the customer think?

... I have been selling GM cars for about fifty years and have been a GM shareholder since 1924 and I feel a hell of a lot more safe in my thirty-five-year-old GM car that has covered 100,000 miles than any new product GM is turning out today. . . ."[173]

IV—TALKERS

It is one of the ironies of history that the man
who built and sold the first automobile radio—and
who made the manufacture of automobile radios
a thriving business—is less likely to be remembered
as a contributer to American industry than as a
largely unappreciated thorn in its side. For fifty
years, David Housman served as president of Automatic Radio Company, competing successfully with
a number of other companies in the manufacture
of radios for specific models of cars. Then, in the
mid-1960s, the sales of his radios began to decline,
for no apparent reason.

There had always been two kinds of companies
in the car radio industry. There were the giant
automobile manufacturers, whose primary business
was making cars, but who also made radios as a
highly lucrative sideline. There were the small independents, who just made radios. In the preceding
few years, however, the independents had begun
to fall by the wayside. Their demise had caused
no great stir; the growing dominance of giant corporations and the decline of small ones was a common trend. By the mid-1960s, however, there were
only two independent radio makers left in competition with the Big Three, and Housman began to
smell a rat. His company had always thrived on
competition, and he refused to believe that the

public was finding his product suddenly less attractive than those of the Big Three, whose sales were growing as rapidly as his own were declining. Yet the retail dealers who had always sold Housman's radios before were now turning them down in favor of expanded shipments from Detroit. When he learned that many of these dealers were changing their orders, not because his radios weren't selling, but because they had been ordered to do so by the manufacturers who granted their franchises, his suspicions turned to outrage.

It did not take Housman long to convince himself that the independent radio manufacturers, along with the independent manufacturers of air conditioners, stereos, and other accessories for new cars, were being made the victims of a conspiracy by the Big Three to eliminate all competitors through the leverage of the auto franchise system. His conviction was highly irreverent, of course—the industry he accused of interfering with free enterprise was the very industry to which free enterprise owed its greatest achievements—and few people took him seriously.

For Housman, whose personal business was threatened, the issue was not an academic one. Having already encountered and survived a number of perils—including those of starting a new business in the twenties, nursing it through the Depression in the thirties, keeping its sales up in the moribund auto market of the forties, and holding his own against flourishing competition in the fifties—he was not about to capitulate without a struggle in the sixties.

Housman's battle with the automobile manufacturers is a classic illustration of the kind of relationship which existed between the manufacturers and their challengers throughout the decade.[174] Of course, his interests during this period were narrower than those of some critics; he was not concerned with broad questions of environmental destruction, the future of cities, and the impact of industry on the quality of life. But the story of his attempts to establish communication with Detroit is the story of nearly everyone who had something unpleasant to discuss with the Big Three in the days when safety, pollution, and congestion were getting to be major issues. The problem for these critics was not that the industry refused to talk, although its refusals were frequent, but that its talk was invariably more concerned with restoring confidence in old virtues than with recognizing urgent new responsibilities. Industry spokesmen tended to treat critics with elaborate condescension, often insinuating that people who were worried about dirty air or burgeoning oligopoly, and who thought that there were any "easy solutions" (meaning solutions which can be implemented *now*), simply did not grasp the realities of American industry. Much fun was made of "tinkerers" who thought they knew of engines which would produce less pollution, or of "idealists" who didn't understand the economics of automobile

production. Most of the critics, it was implied, were
ignorant complainers who were doing a disservice
to the country by arousing public suspicions with
their ill-informed harangues.

David Housman fell quickly into the publicists'
trap. When he spoke, it was plain to see that he
had never been to college. His voice was loud and
uncultured. On the other hand, fifty years as head
of his company had given him confidence both in
the virtues of independence and in the persuasive-
ness of his own salesmanship. Bearing more resem-
blance to an old-fashioned politician on the stump
than to the aging patriarch of a crumbling family
business, he set out to prove that the auto makers
were threatening his existence by infringing on his
right to compete.

What Housman had apparently hoped to make
into a public debate on the rights and rewards of
free enterprise turned out to be a comedy of rhetorical miscarriages. The ingredients for a successful
debate were imminently available: both Housman
and his adversaries (the corporate executives and
public relations mouthpieces of General Motors,
Chrysler, and Ford) were excellent talkers; and the
issue had been popularized by the growing conflict
between big and small business in general. The
trouble was that the hell-for-leather style of Housman, pitted against the creamy-smooth style of the
Big Three representative, resulted in a ludicrous
mismatch. In a Madison Avenue-suckled culture,
creamy-smooth wins every time. And Housman was

not merely outspoken; he seemed to have a great talent for verbal indiscretions, along with an incurable weakness for bombast.

His complaint was simple. In order to make a custom radio (as distinguished from a standard radio which fits any model of car), it is necessary to know the dashboard dimensions of the model for which the radio is being made. The best time to market such radios is during the first couple of months after the new models are introduced, which means that the dimensions must be known several weeks in advance to allow time for tooling up. Housman had asked the makers for these dimensions and they had refused to reveal them. At the same time, they had generously supplied this information to their own subsidiaries, thereby enabling these subsidiaries to monopolize the custom radio market for a substantial part of each year without any competition from outside companies.

The two-month delay of production imposed on him each year by the auto companies was only the beginning. His company was also being shouldered out of the marketplace by a year-round embargo on his radios by independent automobile dealers. Outlets which had been selling Automatic radios for decades were now buying radios only from the subsidiaries of the companies by whom they were franchised to sell new cars.

On June 17, 1968, Housman wrote a letter to GM's James Roche, asking Roche whether he would concede that Automatic Radio Company had a right to compete with GM's Delco in the custom radio market, and, if so, whether he would be kind enough to authorize someone in his company to release the dashboard dimensions necessary to make such competition possible. Housman had written a similar letter the year before and had received a polite brush-off. "Because of the confidential nature of the requested information," Roche had written, "it would be contrary to corporation policy to disclose such information." This time, however, Roche had a good reason to appear somewhat more cooperative. The Small Business Committee of the Senate was planning an investigation of the auto industry, particularly those aspects of the industry which affected small business. Senators Wayne Morse and Gaylord Nelson, chairmen of the Subcommittees on Marketing and Monopoly, had been apprised of Housman's problem and were waiting with considerable interest to see what Roche's reply would be.

The reply succeeded in cutting off relations between General Motors and Automatic altogether, while coolly assuring the Small Business Committee that GM had done nothing wrong. Neither addressed to Housman nor signed by Roche, it came in the form of a brief note from GM counsel Ross Malone to Morse and Nelson. What Housman was asking for, said Malone, "would include complete design parameters including the dimensions from the face of the panel to the firewall, the shape of the mounting braces, the locations of the ashtray and speakers, and the way in which the wiring is mounted and connected. Such information is patently proprietary."

This proved to be something of a red herring. Taking the bait, Housman sent a rambling three-thousand word letter to Nelson and Morse, in which he explained that his company was "not interested in the firewall—or the mounting braces—or the location of the ashtrays—or speakers—or the wiring and connections. Automatic Radio simply wants the measurements of the opening in the dash for the radio and the design of the dash panel, and nothing else." Judging by their previous experience with GM's tactics in public relations, the two senators might have guessed as much. As long as the dialogue between the auto manufacturers and their critics was confined to the obscurity of private correspondence, the issues in question would remain obscured. The manufacturers had already demonstrated their ability to keep legal issues tied up in endless litigation. If the problem of creeping monopoly was a valid one (and they had reasons other than Housman's complaints to believe that it was), it would be dangerous to sit back and expect the problem to be solved by polite negotiations between the shark and the minnow.

Housman had made at least one very salient point: competition in the custom auto radio business was disappearing fast. Small companies which had thrived in an open market were being frozen out by the franchised dealers, who seemed to have less and less freedom to choose which makes of accessory products to sell. Furthermore, Housman's cries (that dealers were being coerced by manufacturers) were being echoed by the dealers themselves. Hundreds of franchisees had complained of increasing intimidation, particularly with respect to the sales of accessory products such as air conditioners and radios. Such sales had always constituted a substantial portion of dealers' profits, and dealers had always been free to choose their own inventories. Now the manufacturers were making decisions which had always been the dealers' prerogative. Products which had once been sold and installed by the dealer were now installed at the factory. Those which dealers were still permitted to install themselves were restricted to the manufacturers' own brands, even though the dealers were supposed to be independent businessmen who could legally sell any brands they wished. Any objections, however, were countered by threats of suspended new-car franchises or delayed new-car shipments. Dealers simply could not afford to risk losing their principal product (new cars) in order to save their other ones. They were forced to capitulate, with the result that a number of companies which had supplied automotive products to dealers were now faced with stacks of canceled orders. Independent custom radio manufacturers had been affected especially severely, with the result that the only ones left in business were Automatic Radio

Company and the Tenna Corporation of Cleveland, Ohio. It was rumored that Tenna was on the rocks, and if Tenna fell that would leave only Automatic to compete with the manufacturers' own subsidiaries. There could be no doubt what the fate of Housman's firm would be.

The mounting urgency of the situation made it clear to the Small Business Committee that the battle of words between the Big Three and its challengers, a battle which amounted to nothing more than an endless and useless stream of verbal sniping and countersniping, would have to be escalated and brought to a head, if any effective action were to be taken before it was too late. It was at least partly on this basis that Nelson and Morse had decided to conduct a series of public hearings in 1968 and 1969. Their intention was to bring together leading critics and defenders of the auto industry to debate a question which preliminary investigations had led them to believe lay at the center of a variety of seemingly disparate but similarly puzzling problems. This was the question of whether planning and regulation were replacing competition in concentrated industries in general, and in the auto industry in particular. Convinced that the Automatic Radio case would have an important bearing on the answer, the committee invited Housman to come to Washington and tell his story. Housman quickly accepted, as did (at a different time) Ralph Nader and several other less known but no less outspoken critics of the automobile manufacturing industry in general.

Bringing about a confrontation proved to be more difficult than the senators had anticipated, however. Auto industry officials are not known for their love of public forums, and in this case they proved even more unavailable than usual. As plans for the first session of the hearings proceeded, it became clear that Roche and his associates in the Big Three were no more interested in discussing their policies with Nader and *his* troublemaking friends than Richard Nixon was in sitting down to chat about the Vietnam War with the leaders of the peace movement. The climate in 1968 and 1969 was not conducive to tolerance of criticism, particularly criticism aimed at establishment policies. Whether in war or in industry, the American establishment of the late 1960s found itself more bitterly excoriated than ever before for its exploitation of the powerless and the poor. It was one of the worst times of the century to ask the silver-haired chairman of General Motors to sit down in a spotlight and allow the policies (and profits) of the most respected company in the land to be questioned by angry dissidents.

Nevertheless, an invitation to Roche was mailed on May 28, 1968. On June 7, Roche wrote back to say that "it would be improper for General Motors to participate in this discussion." The reason, it seemed, was that Nader was still in the process of suing GM for $26 million for invading his privacy after the publication of *Unsafe at Any*

Speed, in which GM was given an embarrassing lambasting for its safety-last approach to automotive design. GM had promptly begun a private "investigation" of Nader, evidently hoping to discover something in his record or behavior that would cast a shadow of doubt over his credibility. Ironically, the investigation resulted in Nader's looking like a paragon of virtue—and GM like an enormous Peeping Tom. In fact, Nader was recently awarded a settlement of $425,000. Nader, it turned out, is a highly ascetic individual who owns no car, lives in a rented room, and avoids conflicts of interest with a passion rarely seen in either Washington or Detroit.

Still smarting from its first two rounds with Nader, GM was evidently in no mood for a third. On the other hand, the Small Business Committee was in no mood to give up its plan. General Motors, Nelson and Morse told themselves humorously, is not the only fish in the sea. A second invitation was sent—this time to Henry Ford II, chairman of the industry's second largest corporation. A reply was presently received from a deputy, Rodney W. Markely, Jr., who said that Mr. Ford was out of the country and that the company's lawyers had advised against participation in the hearing due to "legal difficulties" Ford was having at that time with the federal government. The nature of these difficulties was not explained.

The third invitation went to Thomas C. Mann, president of the Automobile Manufacturers Association and principal apologist for the Detroit establishment. Mann wrote back immediately that he would not participate in the hearing because it had to do with "areas concerning which I have no information and with which the Association may not deal." Similar invitations were dispatched to Chrysler president Virgil E. Boyd, American Motors chairman Roy D. Chapin, and Checker Motors president Morris Markin. All were heard from within a week. Chapin declined on the grounds that his company was too small to represent such a large industry. Markin refused because it would be "impractical for me or any other officer of our corporation to be present at the July 9 hearing." Finally, Chrysler's Boyd said he couldn't come because, after all, it was *General Motors* that this hearing was all about. When Nelson and Morse got their "dialogue" under way a week later, not a single representative of the automobile industry was present to confront Nader (Housman and the others were to appear in the second session).

It was not the first time top auto executives had refused to engage in public dialogue about their public policies, nor was it to be the last. In 1963, for example, the House Committee on Interstate and Foreign Commerce had decided to hold hearings on "Refrigerator Safety Devices," a subject made urgent by a number of household tragedies involving children climbing into refrigerators or deep freezers, closing the doors, and, unable to open the doors from inside, dying of suffocation. The

makers of refrigerators—several of which are subsidiaries of the automobile manufacturing companies—did not appear, and the problem has still not
been solved. The Refrigerator Service Engineers
Society of Chicago, which keeps statistics on the
subject, indicated in 1968 that these deaths were
continuing to increase.[175]

It was at the second session of the Nelson-Morse
hearings in July 1969 that the auto makers finally
agreed to talk. After their initial refusal, pressure
had mounted rapidly. Air pollution had come of
age as a political issue, and the makers found themselves having to placate not just a few powerless
conservationists, but an imposing number of congressmen and administrators as well. Champions
of clean air were itching to introduce strong anti-
automotive legislation. Automotive safety problems were grabbing more headlines than ever, with
callbacks reaching unprecedented numbers. The
death of Corvair came as a grim reminder of the
power of adverse publicity. For the first time in
modern automotive history, independent dealers
were joining forces to resist the manufacturers'
infringements. David Housman was still complaining about the decline of the radio business, and
people were finding they had reason to listen; late
in 1968, Tenna Radio went out of business. The
Big Three were falling from grace, and, from their
point of view, it was high time their fading image
be given a new luster.

When Senator Nelson called a second session of

the auto hearings in 1969 (Morse had lost his seat
in the 1968 election), Roche and the other Big
Three heads again failed to appear, but Thomas
Mann, their trusted public relations specialist, was
appointed to represent them. Conspicuously absent
from the list of witnesses was Nader, who was busy
dragging skeletons from the closets of other industries. Equally conspicuous—by his presence—was
the ruddy-faced Housman, who had waited several
years for this chance.

Housman wasted no words warming up to his
theme. "I come here," he began abruptly, "as a
biased witness to plead . . . for the continuance
of my company's life and the lives of tens of thousands of independent auto accessory manufacturers, all of us victims of (the auto manufacturers')
lust for domination and extermination!"[176] Attack-
ing both the "criminal and monopolistic acts" of
the auto makers and the "ostrichlike" attitudes of
government agencies responsible for controlling
such acts, he first pointed out that the principal
threat to (and destroyer of) businesses like his was
the franchise system of automotive distribution—or
to be more precise, the makers' illegal use of that
system to prevent qualified suppliers from marketing their products through retail dealers. "It is a
naked violation of the Sherman Act," he told the
committee, "for the automobile manufacturers to
thrust their power into the distribution market
through the use of the franchise system. That system has enabled the Big Three to eliminate and

bury independent suppliers and jobbers. The custom radio market bears witness to that fact."

He then waved a document. "Gentlemen, I would like to call your attention to a service manual of Bendix Radio showing all radios manufactured by Bendix for the Ford Motor Company." On the first page appeared the pictures of five radios designed to fit five different cars: the Comet, Galaxie, Mercury, Thunderbird, and Continental. Except for "minor deviations," he said, the five radios were exactly the same. As shown by the schematic diagrams on another page, the five electrical circuits were virtually identical, each using a total of ten transistors and six diodes. Yet the prices charged the franchised dealer by the manufacturer (and passed on to the customer by the dealer) were substantially different.

The prices for radios sold to the dealer ranged from $48.52 for the Comet and Galaxie to $126.07 for the Continental. Prices to the customer for these models were $61.40 and $161.40 respectively, a difference of $100 for essentially the same product. The significance of this difference was not that the Continental was a more expensive car and must therefore be equipped with a more expensive radio. A Continental owner might well be able to afford an accessory of better quality—and therefore of higher price—than the owner of a Comet or Galaxie. Housman had no quarrel with that. The point was that the Bendix radio made for Continental was *not* of significantly better quality than those made for the cheaper cars, irrespective of price.

What concerned Housman was the curious correspondence between the prices charged by Ford and the radios offered for sale by Automatic Radio Company. Automatic sold radios for Comet and Galaxie, but not for Continental. Ford's prices were highly competitive for Comet and Galaxie, but not for Continental. The rub was that Ford didn't *have* any competition in the sales of custom radios for Continental, and could therefore afford to use the excessive profits from its monopolistic sales in one market to subsidize a devastating underselling of its only remaining competition in another.

The same pattern prevailed for all other cars sold on the American market, including the Mercury and Thunderbird shown in the Bendix manual and the entire lines of Chrysler (Motorola) and General Motors (Delco). Automatic Radio and the other independents had never been big enough to tool up every year for every model of car turned out by the prolific mills of the Big Three, and so had been content to produce their radios for just the more popular lines. They had watched helplessly as the Big Three raised its prices—and raked in the profits—on the remaining models.

But there was another frustration, too—the kind of frustration which arises whenever the weak attack the powerful with all the verbal weaponry they can muster—and are answered by implacable silence. It was true that the auto industry had been persuaded to send its representative, Thomas

Mann, to these hearings, and Housman expected that Mann would have much to say when his turn came, despite the fact that he had previously claimed to have "no information" on the subject. But Housman also knew that there were certain topics the auto makers never discussed and that one of these topics was the costs of various manufacturing operations. No figures for the costs of specific models of cars, parts, or accessories (such as radios) were available either to the public or to the government, and as long as the makers had their way, no figures ever would be. While Housman was claiming makers were using excess profits on some models of radios to subsidize price cutting on others, it was widely rumored that similar methods were being used by General Motors to reinforce its control of the lower-price market for cars. In the auto market (as distinguished from the less conspicuous custom radio market), control does not entail the elimination of all competition. General Motors could almost certainly put Ford and Chrysler out of business if it so desired, but GM could not possibly grow much larger than it is already, at least, not in terms of market penetration, without forcing the reluctant hand of the Justice Department's antitrust division.

On the other hand, there is every evidence that GM intends not only to hang on tenaciously to its usual 55 percent of the domestic market, but also to keep this market tightly closed to newcomers. If it is true (as some critics claim) that GM

makes enough profit on Cadillac to keep the prices
on Chevrolet somewhat lower than would be possible if Chevrolet were financed independently, then
it is quite conceivable that GM is using Cadillac
to suppress new entries into the domestic auto
market.[177] Ford and Chrysler, of course, must go
along with GM's prices (which hurt them more
than they hurt GM) in order to protect their own
shares of the pie.

Evidence of such manipulation is necessarily indirect, since direct proof is not possible without
recourse to specific cost data. Though Housman's
testimony strongly suggested that the withering of
competition in custom radios is a symptom of the
same economic disease as the continuing lack of
new competition in the new car market, he was
aware that he could not expose the manufacturers
without cooperation either from the federal government (which had never shown much inclination
to interfere with Detroit's affairs) or—somewhat
improbably—from the manufacturers themselves.[178]

Thomas Mann's appearance at the hearings did
not represent a significant departure from the traditional industry policy of shunning confrontations
with its critics. While precluding repetition of the
previous year's total boycott, which had stirred up
resentment in Congress, Mann could not disguise
the fact that he was no substitute for Roche and
Ford, or for any of dozens of Big Three presidents
and vice presidents with major responsibilities in
the fields of finance, research, and production.

There is more than one way to abort communication, and Mann is a master of the art. The auto industry has its own form of "taking the fifth," as quickly was apparent when it became Mann's turn to speak.

One of the smoothest talkers ever to grace a leather chair, Thomas C. Mann has the credentials of an expert spreader of oil on troubled waters. A lawyer by training, well-tailored, neatly groomed, and distinguished in appearance, he served as Under Secretary of State for Economic Affairs, Assistant Secretary of State for Inter-American Affairs, Assistant Secretary of State for Economic Affairs, Ambassador to El Salvador, and Ambassador to Mexico (among other things) before being spirited away to the Automobile Manufacturers Association in 1967. Addressing the subcommittee on Monopoly in a deep, cultured voice, he began by apologizing in advance for the length of his statement, thereby serving notice that the automobile industry could no longer be accused of shirking its responsibility to communicate fully and frankly with the public.[179] Indeed, the document he was about to read was impressively long and articulate and richly accompanied by pictures and charts.

But first Mann threw in the kicker: "Because of the competitive nature and traditions of (the member companies of the AMA), and because of the requirements of our laws, the Association does not concern itself with what may be properly described as the areas of competition between companies. . . . The Association's interest in these areas is strictly limited to those aspects which are public knowledge and which in no way affect competition. My information on all these subjects is limited to that which is already in the public domain."

During the course of his testimony, especially when questioned by Senator Nelson and Sen. Marlow Cook about some of the stickier areas of auto industry practices, Mann pleaded ignorance no less than sixteen times. On the subject of retail prices, for example, Nelson questioned Mann's assertion that the relatively low prices of 1969 cars (as indicated by the consumer price index) constitutes evidence of "very, very intense competition" among the manufacturers. The Monopoly subcommittee had received substantial evidence that the manufacturers were operating factory outlets at heavy losses in order to increase market penetration, thereby fattening wholesale profits. Nelson wanted to know whether Mann thought this practice could be justified. Mann answered, "I don't have any knowledge about this area, it is unlawful for us to enter into this area as an association, and . . . I speak only from . . . what I get out of reading *Automotive News* and the newspapers." As he spoke, representatives of the manufacturers, who could not have made the same claim of ignorance, sat in the audience fifty feet away, watching the performance of their delegate with obvious satisfaction.

Those issues which most agonized Housman were

viewed with comparative serenity by Mann. While
Housman described the franchise system of auto
distribution as a form of "economic serfdom,"
Mann laughingly declaimed, "I personally know
many dealers who are much wealthier than I am."
While Housman complained that the manufacturers' refusal to tell competing radio companies
the dashboard dimensions of various cars constituted a flagrant antitrust violation, Mann simply
stated, "There is nothing new about the fact that
Gimbel's doesn't tell Macy's. Automotive companies are no more secretive about their internal data
than other industries, and perhaps less so than
most."

This last was one of Mann's more masterful comments, insofar as it killed two very annoying birds
with one rhetorical stone. In the first place, it
conveniently obliterated any distinction between
(a) a company which must sell its product (car
radios) through a distribution system controlled by
its principal competitor, and (b) a company which
controls the distribution of both its own product
(cars) *and* its competitors' products (car radios),
simply by virtue of the fact that its own products
are the most important ones sold by the distributors—and the ones the distributors would be least
willing to lose in a battle between different suppliers. Macy's survival does not depend on its capacity
to sell products which can only be used as accessories to Gimbel's products and which can only be
sold in Gimbel's stores.

In the second place, by suggesting that auto companies may be *less* secretive than other industries, Mann's comment seemingly made a virtue of something that antitrust authorities have traditionally considered a serious vice. Once the basic information necessary for competition to exist has been made available to all would-be competitors, any additional exchange of information is viewed with considerable suspicion. During the 1960s, critics of the auto industry frequently noted that whereas the Big Three yielded very little information to outsiders, they also kept very few secrets from each other. Thus, when GM vice president Semon Knudson moved across Detroit to become president of Ford, both companies acknowledged that Ford gained no competitive advantage (Knudson was subsequently fired). Had Mann been more concerned with accuracy than with rhetorical neatness, he might have noted that whereas Gimbel's doesn't tell Macy's, Ford doesn't tell the independent auto accessory manufacturers (or the public) but *does* tell GM and Chrysler and even American Motors Corporation.

In many ways, the differences between Thomas Mann and David Housman epitomized the industry's general unresponsiveness to complaints it simply could not appreciate. Failures in communication, caused by the hopeless interaction between deliberate sophistry and blatant anger, resulted in a ten-year tragicomedy of mutual frustration. Confrontations invariably pitted polished professional equivocators against amateur "tell-it-like-it-is" types, neither of whom seemed able, or willing, to comprehend the other. The industry, thoroughly enamored of the affluence it had brought both to the country and to itself, could not understand what all the fuss was about. Critics, angered by the industry's insensitivity to a growing catalogue of problems, became more and more impatient with the tendency of Detroit to substitute words for actions. Immediate action was needed, they said, to clean the air, stop the slaughter, reduce the costs, clear the congestion, and restore vitality to the whole industry. To Mann, whose record suggested that he had never really worried about such things (his job is to spread the gospel of super-productiveness), Housman's testimony was foolish and annoying. To Housman, Mann's aloofness—his unwillingness to acknowledge the urgency of the independent suppliers' plight—represented nothing more than the hired voice of a hypocritical monopoly.

The endless equivocation with which Housman was forced to cope could not be attributed to the relative unimportance of Automatic Radio Company. Anyone else who questioned the industry's practices, whether he was a United States Senator or a leading economist, was likely to receive the same kinds of evasive assurances. For all its glibness, the record of the automobile industry's pronouncements in the 1960s reveals a considerable lack of real assurance. Statements tended to be peremptory, yet defensive. Public relations were obviously stopgap in nature, designed only to smooth over each embarrassing situation as it arose, rather than to implement a larger policy. The result, for those who looked closely, was an endless series of contradictions. When Henry Ford thought he could get away with it, he sneered at the air pollution problem. Yet, a year later when environment was a sexy issue, Ford expressed deep concern.[180] While the National Air Pollution Control Administration was showing devastating effects of automotive pollution in every state, an automotive writer who generally functions as a mouthpiece for Detroit blithely announced "There is no evidence to link the automobile to these problems."[181] While America slumbered in its ignorance of pollution, the industry did nothing to alleviate it—for fifty years. But when the law clamped down in 1968 and insisted that crude control devices be attached to cars, James Roche began sounding like a Russian historian. "We did the pioneering work in parts-per-million (pollution concentration) chemistry starting in the 1920s," he announced.[182] (Since the National Education Association has estimated that the total sum of man's scientific knowledge has been doubling every ten years orso,[183] it is hard to imagine what the auto industry was doing with itself in the four decades since, according to Roche, it started "work" on pollution!) Three months later, he dismissed the whole problem of physiological danger with a masterful bit of rhetoric: "We know there is some (danger), but scientists debate how much. Meanwhile we act."[184] The picture of scientists wasting precious time while GM forged ahead was a perfect inversion of actual roles. When debate centered on the relative merits of steam and internal combustion cars, makers called the internal combustion car "simple."[185] But when the debate swung to the question of why there were so many callbacks, they were suddenly "enormously complex."[186] While studies showed that streets are so strangled by cars that traffic moves more slowly than it did before carriages became horseless, Ford president Knudson, in a deft bit of doubletalk, claimed that "the auto actually has been the greatest single contributor toward relieving traffic congestion."[187]

Some of the most blatant equivocations concerned the nature of big business. "Many who deplore the bigness of business mistake economic competition for the predatory life of the jungle, where the big grow bigger as the small grow fewer," said Roche in 1968. "This is not the case . . . a century ago about 300,000 businesses served a population of 29 million. Today 4.8 million serve a population of 200 million. So, while population has grown seven-fold, the number of businesses has multiplied sixteen times."[188]

Perhaps it was just Roche's habit of equating bigger with better that tempted him to characterize a bigger number of businesses with a better business environment. More likely, Roche simply preferred to draw attention away from the really pertinent statistics, which show that while the number of businesses has increased, the *share* of the market held by these businesses has shifted steadily to the giant ones like Roche's own GM.' In 1947, companies other than the two hundred largest accounted for 70 percent of total output; by 1963 their proportion had fallen to 59 percent. In 1950, the two hundred giants had 47 percent of total manufacturing assets. By 1965, their share had risen to 55 percent. According to Dr. Willard Mueller, former chief economist of the Federal Trade Commission, by 1975 the two hundred largest corporations will control two-thirds of manufacturing assets if the present trend continues.[189] Yet Roche was willing to announce that the growth of big business "has not occurred at the expense of small business."

Such patchwork public relations reflects a long-time disinclination of the auto industry to put the significance of its work into broad perspective. That the makers are accomplished talkers is apparent from the fact that they always have a ready excuse for anything that goes wrong. That they are dangerously small thinkers is evident in the fact that the things they say reflect no consistent philosophy of business, no overriding goals other than to get off the hook and go back to production. This weakness has long been characteristic of Detroit, as indicated for example in *My Years With General Motors,* the autobiography of Alfred Sloan. Reviewing the book for *Fortune,* Peter Drucker wrote,

"Not one general idea is developed in the book, and there are no explicitly stated convictions. Sloan built the biggest manufacturing business of all times. He defended it against attacks on "bigness" and antitrust suits. Yet hardly a word is said in the book about big business, its place in society and the economy, its responsibilities, its policies."[190]

It is said that two lies must be told to cover one. How many of the absurdities proffered by Detroit are conscious violations of truth, as distinguished from statements which are misleading but technically true, is hard to say and in any case hardly matters. "A truth that's told with bad intent beats all the lies you can invent," says the proverb. In any case, by 1970 so many questionable things were being said that even the most polished of professional talkers found themselves tripping up. At times, the chairman of General Motors resembled the little boy who, when accused of hitting another little boy, said, "I did not—and besides, he hit me first." When the *Michigan Daily* published its alleged proof of an antilabor conspiracy among the Big Three, Roche took one look at the document and said "I don't know where this came from. I don't know what it is. Whatever it is, it is a confidential document and somebody stole it."

V—BUYERS

It is a sad manifestation of the utter incredibility of American advertising that General Motors can tell the country "GM SETS THE STYLE"—and get away with it. The point is not that the statement is false, but that it is absolutely, brazenly true. It is so true that if people really believed what they read, GM could never permit such an advertisement to appear. GM sets the style so compellingly that no other domestic manufacturer dares to try anything different. This, in itself, is enough to put a strain on the table conversation when the Department of Justice (Antitrust Division) drops in for dinner.

But GM does not merely set styles in cars; it also has an inordinate influence on the style of life of their owners. The preoccupation with size, power, and potency which pervades American life is symbolized by the American car, and the symbol is both chicken and egg to the thing symbolized. To some extent, of course, cars merely reflect the values that people already have. But cars, or the people who design them, also shape and reinforce these values. When a GM commercial shows a new car gliding across a lyrical southwestern landscape while a youthful voice sings "The Big Rider is Impala," it is only capitalizing on the current popularity of the movie "Easy Rider." But when cars with tailfins sell beautifully in 1960 and don't sell at all in 1970, that isn't because some mysterious shift in public attitudes has made tailfins go out of style. It is because the *makers* have made them go out of style. As much as anyone else, it is the auto stylist who determines what is attractive and what is ugly in the United States.

In the prevailing style at the beginning of the 1970s, the greatest beauty was youth. The younger a car, the more desirable. Oldsmobile, in the tradition of Cinderella's pumpkin, suddenly became a "youngmobile," and every new car was deemed *by definition* more beautiful than last year's model.[191] All this was just fine with the manufacturers, since nothing delights Detroit quite like the customer who tires of his new car after a few months and promptly gets a wandering eye for something else. It was not until after World War II that the makers began to discover all the little things they could do to make *everyone* get tired of his car in a hurry, but since then they have improved on the techniques with every passing year. It is not uncommon these days for the new-car owner to be thoroughly disenchanted with his purchase by the time he gets it home from the showroom.

The makers have two basic methods of speeding up the natural processes by which people decide to trade in their old cars for new ones. One is psychological obsolescence, the unwillingness of the owner to endure the car. The other is technological obsolescence, the apparent unwillingness of the car to endure its owner. Psychological obsolescence is promulgated by advertising, factory-sponsored racing and word of mouth. It acts like a massive hormonal injection, causing the entire population to become unnaturally impatient with the passing of time. Often, the purchase of a car resembles the attempt of a woman past her prime to make herself younger by wearing a girl's clothes. Technological obsolescence simply reinforces psychological obsolescence by causing the car to fall apart just when its owner is on the verge of overcoming his own whimsies.

One cruel irony of automotive advertising is that it achieves its purposes by making promises no car can fulfill. Because it teases constantly, it never satisfies—and its readers remain eternally hungry. For the young, it paints false pictures of youth, thereby encouraging millions of young people to believe their own experience is abnormal. An ad showing a curvaceous Mercury Cyclone surrounded by teenage males tells its readers, "We made it hot. You can make it scream."[192] The ad does not merely encourage dangerous and illegal driving; it also represents—can anyone help reading between the lines?—a gross perversion of normal sexuality.

A GM ad tells the reader he will have "an almost neurotic urge to get going." Another ad tells its potential driver to "Drive it like you hate it." A Chevy ad claims "Nobody said a nice car can't play mean now and then."[193] The gospel of Detroit is full of such incitements to physical and moral violence. The Big Three and their advertisers are among the most prolific purveyors of obscene literature in America. Yet people who are worried about the effects of Picasso nudes or sex education diagrams on their children have been blinded to the effects of automotive advertising.

Restless people searching for gratifications cars promise but can't deliver, like drug addicts who know their lives are empty but still can't resist perpetuating the illusion of happiness drugs convey, have powerful incentives to buy new cars. There is no *proof* that the makers' advertising has any impact at all, but what else explains the lemming-like trek of American consumers to the showrooms each fall? Even taking into account the rapid deterioration of today's cars, the car is one of the most overconsumed commodities in America, where overconsumption—of food, drugs, drinks, toys, neckties—is both a national compulsion and an entrenched institution. Yet there is little real evidence that the average driver's feeling for his new automobile amounts to anything much more than a temporary infatuation. A new-car affair which starts off with a surge of ego-involvement is likely to turn quickly to sour impatience as the fenders become nicked and dented and the body falls out of style within months of its purchase. There are exceptions; one article in *Life* told of a retired engineer whose affection for his 1923 Rolls Royce, "Don Quixote," is so deep that he speaks of the car as if it were his only son ("He has started getting punctures . . . He is a difficult car"). But most exceptions are, like "Don Quixote," classic cars built years before the idea of an annual model change and a mass arbitrary conditioning of public responses to carefully disseminated aesthetic stimuli ever crept into the collective mind of the manufacturers. Now, in a love-them-and-leave-them spirit, Americans buy nine million new cars a year and throw seven million away, many of them still in running condition.

In such behavior there are signs of contempt, as well as of infatuation. Whether contempt is a symptom of underlying resentment or just a modern manifestation of traditional American pragmatism (in a super-productive economy it may pay to waste) is not clear. Americans have always thought of themselves as pragmatists, especially in matters of gadgets and machines. Fixing cars became a national pastime with the advent of the Model T Ford, which came closer in its popularity to making a favorite old moneylender's fantasy come true ("I'll give you a hundred dollars today if you'll give me a penny today, two cents tomorrow, four cents the next day, and just keep doubling the amount each day for a month") than any other major product since the beginning of the Industrial Revolution. Henry Ford I managed to almost double his sales every year for eight consecutive years after the Model T was introduced. By the time the boom leveled off (or to be more precise, by the time it settled down to a more sedate expansion),

there was a Ford in every backyard and somebody—the owner, his neighbor, a son, or the friend
of a son, but not a professional mechanic—was
working on the engine or polishing the fender. The
high school years were more for learning about cars
than any other subject (except maybe girls, who
usually had something to do with the cars), and
car-knowledge accrued to the young American male
as naturally as baseball statistics and food.

Today, for all the proliferation of cars in the
United States, this is no longer true. Cars have
lost much of their appeal to the average backyard
mechanic, if not to his wife and unmechanically
minded son, who drives around the neighborhood
like Parnelli Jones but has to go to a gas station
if he wants to have his oil changed. A possible
factor, of course, is the increasing complexity of
cars. "The modern automobile requires a skilled
technician to make even a minor adjustment," says
a senior editor of *Machine Design*.[194] But another
answer may be that cars simply don't appeal—
aren't made to appeal—to the pragmatic nature of
men as they did once.

Yet the public is as schizophrenic about finding
fault with the auto industry as the government is.
For most Americans the threshold of indignation,
especially about cars, is very high. Many consumers
seem either unaware of the fact that the cars they
drive are unnecessarily expensive and destructive,
or utterly unconcerned about it. Several studies
bear this out, including a monumental survey of

transportation attitudes and behavior, jointly un-
dertaken in 1968 by the Highway Research Board
of the National Academy of Sciences, the Bureau
of Public Roads, and the American Association of
State Highway Officials. One question in particular
was designed to show just how reluctant people
are to find fault with cars. A representative sample
of American drivers was reminded that "the automobile pollutes the air and creates traffic congestion. Highway development demolishes homes and
often destroys previously attractive landscapes.
The increasing number of automobiles, together
with inadequate highways, kill over fifty thousand
people every year. In your opinion, is the contribution the automobile makes to our way of life worth
this?" The question was asked by two independent
research organizations, each using its own sample.[195] Of those questioned, 84.7 percent of one sample and 84.2 percent of the other answered "yes."
Questioned further as to why they thought cars
are "worth it," the respondents offered a large variety of reasons, the most common one being that
"the auto is the only form of transportation available."

These results were corroborated by a rather puzzling experiment conducted in Flint, Michigan, in
1969. The city's 100,000 commuters were provided
with the most accommodating alternative to automotive transportation anyone could wish—or so
it was thought. The alternative consisted of an
elaborate door-to-door bus service, complete with

stereo music, air conditioning, and stewardesses. In the evening, some of the buses even stopped in at the local tavern, in accordance with their passengers' habits, before dropping them off at home. The result? Nearly everyone continued driving his car, as usual.[196]

Both studies suggest that the odds are heavily against any alternatives to cars gaining widespread public acceptance in the near future. Yet it is probably worth noting that the Highway Research Board study turned up a small but not insignificant minority of drivers who do *not* believe cars are "worth it," as long as they continue to "do the things they do." For this group 15 percent is probably too large a figure, since the survey question was given a deliberate "bias" by the researchers in order to minimize the number of "yes" answers, thereby enhancing the significance of those which occurred. The importance of the 15 percent who answered "no" must not be overemphasized, since some of these may have been swayed by the negative slant of the question. On the other hand, evidence from other sources indicates that this figure may not be far out of line. The number of Americans who have had parents, children, relatives or friends killed or crippled in auto accidents; or who have simply grown sick and tired of paying inflated amounts of money for minor repairs and invisible adjustments; or who have had their insurance abruptly canceled by a company which pretends to wish it were out of the auto insurance business altogether; or who have reached the end of their rope with the infuriating business of crawling home ten feet at a time for forty-five minutes every night—the number of people who are no longer willing to accept the premise that all these dangers and frustrations are necessary, has reached into the millions and perhaps tens of millions. Many Americans have not understood that accidents and smog and high costs and congestion are not necessary and inevitable, and so they have suffered in silence. They have always believed that accidents are caused by bad driving, a belief which is firmly rooted in the puritanical proclivity to feel guilty about everything that goes wrong in one's life, and which is carefully nurtured by the automobile industry. Until Nader published *Unsafe at Any Speed* in 1965, it rarely occurred to anyone that the accident rate may be a function, not only of the number of people who mix drinking and driving, but also of the miniscule percentage of its enormous profits General Motors sets aside—or neglects to set aside—for basic safety research and engineering.

Similarly, it was not very hard a few years ago to convince oneself that rush hour congestion was the commuter's own fault for living in the suburbs and working downtown, or for trying to go home at the same time as everyone else. Now some erstwhile defeatists are changing their minds and deciding that other factors, such as the amount of federal money set aside for highways at the expense of mass transit, or simply the size and shape of their cars, are at least equally significant. (As *Saturday Review's* Norman Cousins declared in 1967, "An automobile takes up space in defiance of all the logic that pertains to the operation of a large community. Moreover the passion of designers to make cars look like frankfurters has resulted in front seats that require a unnatural sitting position and rear seats that make human legs an encumbrance. A long protrusion jutting far out over the rear wheels represents an ultimate tribute to baggage but makes parking the business of the devil. The net effect of this squeezed-out design is to reduce by one-third to one-half the number of cars that can pass a heavily trafficked point within a given time. . . .".[197] Seen from this critical perspective, none of the financial and environmental problems generally associated with cars and highways are immune to change.

Few customers have ever bothered to strike back at the causes of their miseries, however. For those devastated by tragedy, such as the family of a Huntsville, Alabama, boy who was killed when the brakes on his school bus failed, it is too late for prevention and impossible to obtain retribution. The offer of Chevrolet's chief engineer to help the Huntsville community work out a maintenance program for its school buses (thereby suggesting that the failure had been due to poor maintenance rather than to defective parts made by General Motors) could not have been much comfort to the family.[198] For those frustrated by lesser troubles, the toil and expense of complaints or lawsuits merely add more trouble to the troubles they already have. Private citizens who sue the auto industry for "failing to clean up smog" are rare exceptions to the prevailing attitude that it just isn't "worth it" to struggle. Often, as with the daily "rush"-hour crawl, the determining factor is inertia. Drivers will tolerate great inconveniences rather than break the routines of their lives, just as they will often drive half a mile around the block rather than stop and turn around in a driveway.

This ambivalence, which has added an element of suspense to the drama of the automotive struggle (both Washington and Detroit are confused by the crosscurrents) has come about partly because the interests of drivers and those of the public are both very much the same and very different. On one hand, nearly all Americans old enough to drive—about 115 million—are now licensed as drivers.[199] To a large extent, therefore, the interests of the public and those of the drivers of cars are identical. Thus, it has often been assumed (in studies to determine the need for new highways through residential areas, for example) that what is good for drivers is good for America. On the other hand, to say that most adult Americans are drivers is not at all the same as to say that adult Americans spend most of their time driving. When a driver gets out of his car, he ceases to be a driver and his interests change, often quite radically. He may suddenly find himself in the position of a pedestrian, thoroughly annoyed by the noise, fumes, and rudeness of drivers, and frustrated by the special status accorded to cars. In Washington, D.C., pedestrians are frequently ticketed for getting into the way of cars, but cars drive through orange and red lights with impunity. "Washington policemen," a *Washington Post* reader wrote in a letter to the editor, "are afraid of automobiles and vent their frustration by stopping pedestrians. Regardless of 'Walk' and 'Don't Walk' signs, no driver has the right to turn into crosswalks without regard for pedestrians. What Washington needs is a department for pedestrians to combat the present Department of Highway and Traffic which is solely interested in speeding the movement of automobiles. Both the Police and Traffic Department forget that almost everyone is a pedestrian part of the time. Everyday automobile commuters make more pedestrian trips than automobile trips."[200]

In some sections of New York City, pedestrians are so numerous at certain hours of the day that they overflow the sidewalks and completely occupy the streets, turning cars into helpless islands of hornblowing frustration. Neither drivers' curses nor policemen's tickets are the slightest deterrent to the walkers, who have made it clear that cars are not only no longer wanted in such areas, they are no longer even *recognized*. As anthropologist Edward T. Hall has often noted, human beings require a minimum amount of space in which to live and move, the boundaries of which are quite independent of actual physiological needs.[201] If the "canyons" of the financial district of New York are so confining that crowds of people must walk in the street *simply because they are people,* then walk in the street they will, risks of fines or drivers' wrath notwithstanding.

Despite the fact that the automobile industry cannot be expected to profit in the long run by inflicting its product on the living space of its customers, the inner city struggle between cars and people has continued relentlessly—with people the gradual losers. In the central business district of Milwaukee, for example, planning has been so auto-oriented that cars have been enabled to move through and around the area with extraordinary freedom. But the price has been the mobility of pedestrians, for whom the area has taken on the character of what one urban designer calls "negative congestion."[202] Since the area has become both physically and psychologically hostile to anyone without a car, pedestrian traffic has dwindled. Stores, like cells of an organism suffering from poor circulation of the blood, have languished. Ironically, the effect can be just as debilitating when streets do *not* facilitate the movement of vehicles, simply because circulation of both cars and pedestrians then slows to a worm's pace, which is as bad for local business as if there were very little circulation at all.

Pedestrians constitute just one of many categories of people whose needs are different from those of drivers, and who find their interests being more and more encroached on by the 100 million cars which now dominate the landscape. There are also parents who want safe places for children to play, and such places grow scarcer by the day. (Of the eleven thousand pedestrians struck and killed by cars each year, a large number are children who are unable to get off their roller skates or tricycles in time. . . .). And then there are those people who find pleasure in silence and in the subtle sounds of the natural world—of wind and water and wild-life—but who are compelled to live in places where the penetrating sound (and smell) of gasoline engines fills the air to the exclusion of anything natural. These groups of people probably constitute significant segments of the American population. There are also hundreds of smaller groups whose interests are directly opposed to those of drivers, but whose survival depends on the whims of an auto lobby that is largely oblivious to their existence. Bicyclists, for example, need roads as much as cars do, but their safety and pleasure are so threatened by the drivers for whom the roads were built that the two-wheeler has been virtually extinguished as a form of transportation. (Even kids have given up on bikes, except as pieces of fancy acrobatic equipment more suited to doing handlebar tricks in a driveway than riding on a road.) In some European cities, bicycles rival cars as a mode of transportation, taking far less space than cars, requiring no fuel, producing no pollution, and keeping their owners considerably more fit. In American cities, frustrated drivers blow their horns angrily at bicyclists, apparently resentful that anything not powered by a large gasoline engine—even though bikes have proved *faster* than cars in downtown areas—[203]should have the temerity to seek a share of the road.

Drivers, in their attitude toward all who get in their way, whether they be children, bicyclists, joggers, or other drivers, seem to embody the policies of the auto and highway interests which made them. Athletes who keep fit by running on roads (in snowy winter and muddy spring, there is often nowhere else to go) say they are not infrequently harassed by drivers who let forth with loud obscenities, punctuated by long blasts of the horn, and who frequently swerve directly toward the runner to drive him off, sometimes from the opposite side of the road. Hikers have similar problems with cars; the Appalachian Trail, a two-thousand mile footpath which wends its way through wilderness areas from Maine to Georgia, is being increasingly crossed by highways. These highways present a considerable hazard to weary hikers, yet the builders of the highways have never bothered to provide crossing assistance. In at least one place, the trail has been obliterated by road-builders, who have found the ridges of mountains profitable places to lure drivers.[204] Drivers are thus pushing hikers out of the remotest spots, and are also pushing people out of the densest urban areas.

Thousands of homes are condemned annually to make room for new highways. Such highways are built for the convenience of drivers, not for the well-being of the cities they disrupt and entangle. The "driver" lobby, supported by the juggernaut of the auto, oil, and highway industries, is always more powerful than the little groups of people it deposes. Yet, ironically, one reason for the power of the driver interests is the fact that virtually every conservationist, hiker, pedestrian, jogger, bicyclist, worried mother, and urban dweller is also the driver of a comfortable American automobile.

For many drivers, ambivalence about cars is heightened by occupational loyalties. As the Automobile Manufacturers' Association delights in pointing out, some fourteen million persons, which constitute about 16 percent of the total working force in the United States, work in the manufacture, distribution, maintenance and commercial use of motor vehicles. The result is a mass conflict of interest between social responsibility and personal security. Many of those who are already torn between the conveniences and annoyances of cars are further aggravated by fears that changes in the car's role would in some way jeopardize their jobs. These fears are often unfounded; some are carefully nurtured by the auto interests, but they nevertheless constitute a formidable political force.

Beyond all this, there is one other factor which makes individual drivers dubious representatives of the public interest. The fact that cars are risky and costly does not necessarily alienate the people who own them, many of whom apparently consider the absurdities of new cars virtues rather than deficiencies. Thus, while there are some who evaluate cars only in terms of functional qualities, there are millions of others for whom the nonfunctional characteristics the very traits for which fatalities, congestion, and expense are blamed are most desirable.[205] In this respect, the car has a remarkable symbolic power, reflecting (whether by cause or by effect) the attitudes of its users, much as the artists of an era reflect such attitudes in their work.

Americans have long been known for their pragmatism, and for several decades pragmatic considerations determined the design of cars. This is not to say that the early cars weren't very sexy, nor is it to say the fulfillment of aesthetic or psychological needs is not a valid function. In the Golden Age of Greece, the Parthenon was a very functional building, insofar as the religious needs of the Athenians required specific architectural features. The early car in America, however, for all its lovability, was built to meet more mundane requirements. It had to haul people, provide space for groceries, and hold itself together against the ravages of rural winters and rutted roads. It was built primarily for the American farmer, an economy-minded fellow who regarded a car as a piece of equipment which, like a hoe or a pump, either did its job or didn't. In subsequent years, the farmer traded his car for a pickup truck, while the car moved to the city and suburbs. The prevailing relationship between Americans and their cars became noticeably more esoteric.

Running at crosscurrents to the pragmatism in the American blood is a heady stream of romanticism, the proclivity to react *against* rationality. Such proclivities become particularly urgent when institutions, like schools and governments—the nerve centers of rational activity—become so rigid that rationality becomes a life-denying principle. When people become bored with their lives because the institutions they are constantly feeding now seem to exist only for the purpose of meaningless self-perpetuation, the times are ripe for romantic revolution. People begin to search for means of escape from the vicious circle of what seems to them a meaningless existence. In the 1960s, the symptoms became acute; young people reached unprecedented levels of restlessness, while older people were torn between frustration with their own failure to make things right, and anger with their children for being so unappreciative. Few of these people, either the restless young or the frustrated old, were looking for safe, practical, pleasant little cars in which to drive around.

The "escape machines," as GM called some of its cars in 1970, are not the only means of escape available to Americans. Drugs, yoga, zen, incense, alcohol, music, wife-swapping, suicide, dressing up like Indians, and even killing "Commies" in far-off jungles all became, between 1960 and 1970, increasingly popular means by which Americans shook off the pedestrian routines and spiritual dullness of their lives. For "middle America," however, many of these activities were unacceptable. Only the car and the war had the advantages of being institutions themselves, thereby easing the moral burden on those who felt a conflict between the need to escape and the need to be "normal" and "law-abiding" citizens. Thus, in the 1960s, the very concept of "law and order" became intimately bound up with the "hawk" position on war, despite the fact that war is the most lawless, disorderly activity ever engaged in by man; and the related concept of the "normal" citizen became that of the driver of a new oversized, overpowered, oversexed American car, replete with pseudo-weapons on the nose—and an American flag in the window. People who took "trips" on drugs were liable to be considered deviant, but who could possibly impugn the normality of people who took trips in Oldsmobiles? The miracle of the escape machine is that it enabled people to have their institutional cake and eat it too. As one high-flying car-nut wrote in the June 1969 issue of *Motor Trend:*

Only a machine like the Hurst/Olds can do it; a hoodscooped, panel-painted, mag-wheeled, trunk-spoilered antidote for our uptight anonymous world. Your car is you or the Walter Mitty dream of you your mind has on instant, stop-action replay. It is the natural law for youth that a groovy guy always owns a groovy car and if you've got the car, groovy chicks will be in it. The Hurst/Olds is a money-back guarantee. And it is also an insurance policy against premature old age, like studded snow tires to keep you from sliding down the icy slope on the shaded side of 30.[206]

Romance in cars, like that in other art forms, is manifested in several forms. Thus it may be a reaction against an overfamiliar world (let's have more dreaming!) or an overprotective lifestyle (more danger!). The overfamiliar world, to borrow an observation from Marshall McLuhan, is one of the pervasive effects of a media-dominated culture. TV, radio, and film have turned the globe into one big, unhappy village! There are no more mysterious places. Russia and Africa and even the moon are as familiar to us as our own sinks. Ironically, physical transportation serves the same functions on a continental scale that communication serves globally. The mobility of the car has considerably diminished the attractiveness of the "other side of the mountain," which we now know looks pretty much like this side. In the past, those bored with the immediacy of their surroundings could dream of the faraway and long ago. Today, in America, there is no "faraway," and the country is too young for a long ago (except for those who put on their beads and play Indian). Dreamers must turn inward instead of outward. Some recede into their "heads." Others climb into cars, which (aha!) have much to offer beside physical mobility. At least, so one gathers from the commercials which picture cars gliding through bucolic landscapes and perched like eagles on sunstruck mesas. The world of the driver, as depicted by Madison Avenue, is as mystical and dreamlike as the pleasure dome of Kubla Khan.

The overprotective culture is a particularly American phenomenon. For the middle-class male, there are virtually no physical dangers left; no need to kill wolves, hunt for meat, or defend the village from marauding savages. The amount of power wielded is greater than ever (mostly sublimated in memos and board meetings) but the risks are as buffered as the contests. We are constantly exposed to *stories* of risk in our endless reading and viewing, but the greatest risk of death most Americans ever undertake is to drive a powerful car.

Detroit is fully aware of the psychological implications of the car and collaborates fully with the needs of its drivers. The result is a business far more thriving than transportation needs alone could satisfy. Few ads emphasize transportation. Most emphasize either the druglike effect of a car on its occupants or the *dangerous* quality of the car. When safety became a "hot" issue in the late 1960s, narcosis became the thing. "Turn on with Ford," invited the makers in one widely-circulated ad. But other ads continued to appeal to the angry and the frustrated—those who find release in aggression and risk.[207]

The most salient characteristic of a car is the

fact that it is controlled entirely by the driver. This, more than anything else, is what makes a car a car, what distinguishes it from a train, or a plane, or even a taxi. Drivers have often, in polls and interviews, tried to articulate powerful feelings involved in this control. A common explanation has been that one can go anywhere one wants, at any time. Certainly, this is important. But such control means something else as well; it means the driver holds, literally in the palm of his hands, both his own life and the lives of his fellow creatures. No other situation gives the average man such arbitrary power over life. One of the principal risks of driving, quite aside from the risk of pure accident (Is there any such thing as a pure accident?), is the extraordinary responsiveness of this power to the momentary impulses of man. A driver who is angry or frustrated (for whatever reason) can step on the gas and *instantly* the world around him changes in response to his feelings. The decisiveness and irrevocability of this response create a special temptation to the inhabitants of a world which has become slower and slower to respond to any single gesture, and where the anger of the president himself must be blunted, diffused, filtered, and processed before its effects can be much felt.

Thus, it is perhaps not control *per se* which makes for the fascination of a powerful car, but control of a kind which leaves the driver unprotected from the consequences of his own acts; for while there are many kinds of control men still wield over their own lives, society has built an elaborate fail-safe system for the errant behavior of most of its unluckier members. A man who cannot keep a job because he is willful is not likely to be allowed to starve; willy-nilly, a government agency, a relative, or a good Samaritan will feed him. If he gets sick, he will probably be treated whether he wants treatment or not. Society is full of institutions calculated to break one's fall. It is, therefore, virtually impossible to fall *all the way,* and so it is impossible to take into one's hands the kind of responsibility which produces a full sense of the simultaneous power and fallibility which makes a human being what he is.

There are thousands of cases on record of motorists yielding to sudden impulses—even whims—which proved to be their utter undoing. A random example; on May 3, 1969, a driver in Austin, Texas, "apparently angered" by hippies who "pounded and hopped on his car" when he tried to drive through the street where they were holding an unauthorized dance, backed up three blocks, drove forward at full speed, and smashed into the crowd. Then he did it again. Thirty-three of the dancers required hospitalization. One week later a similar crowd was attacked by a like-minded motorist in Zap, North Dakota.

Most drivers, of course, are horrified at such behavior. At the same time, it has often been noted that driving "brings out the worst in human nature," that people "take out their aggressions" in driving, and so on. While the overt use of the car as a weapon is exceptional, smaller (and *usually* less consequential) acts of impulse are not. There may be a little-recognized importance in such acts, insofar as they give drivers the opportunity to dare "fate," to confront the flaws of their own character and judgment, and still survive. How many drivers risk their lives, again and again, to pass a single car and gain a forty-foot advantage on a crowded two-lane road? Not to give play to such flaws, it might be argued, is not to be fully sensitive to the essential distinction between one's self, a mortal and foolhardy and not entirely rational organism, and the machines of which one's environment increasingly consists.

That modern men should relish the chanciness of their own existence, provided the chances they take proceed from their own actions, is illustrated by a recent study of the "values" of various kinds of risks to which people are subjected. According to the M.I.T. *Technology Review,* Dr. Chauncey Starr of the University of California (L.A.) School of Engineering and Applied Science has felt that it would be possible to demonstrate "rough quantitative relationships between the risks of death to which people expose themselves—in driving, smoking, flying, mining, waging war—and the values they place on these activities, measured in dollars." Measuring the dollar value of a "voluntary" activity in terms of what the individual pays to engage in it, and that of an "involuntary" activity in terms of the contribution it makes to the average annual income, Dr. Starr compared a wide range of human activities and came to the remarkable conclusion that "people are prepared to expose themselves voluntarily to about a thousand times the danger they will tolerate from the actions of others."[208]

In 1923, D. H. Lawrence, expressing the need for a theater of life which enables man to be whole not only in his self-control but also in his fallibility, his anger, his urges, wrote:

> The perfectibility of man! Ah heaven, what
>   a dreary theme!
> The perfectibility of the Ford car![209]

But that was in the days when Ford cars were used primarily for transportation.

VI—WHAT'S GOOD FOR GM . . .

To understand the impact of cars and their makers on the quality of American life, it is necessary first to dispel any notion of the Big Three as an "enemy"—or of their product as a kind of Midas' gold with which we have enriched ourselves to the point of cultural starvation. The car is not a disguised evil so much as a misdirected good. Its makers are not villains so much as tarnished heroes. Their failings are a direct consequence of virtuous traits developed to a pathetic extreme. They are, for the most part, patriotic men who would do nothing consciously to weaken their country or its people, but part of their problem is that they are not quite sure what their country really *is*. They are well trained in the economics of money, but feel much less at ease, as do most Americans, with the economics of things which can never be exchanged in a marketplace.

For half a century, the "costs" of cars and highways were defined purely in terms of money and time, while the "benefits" of these things were defined in terms of money and time saved. The concept of "social costs," popularized in the late 1960s, only made the makers defensive. What *was* a social cost? And who was to pay it?

Clearly, the social costs of cars included the costs of automotive by-products, which in the past had simply been ignored. The difficulty of evaluating the impact of even so definable a by-product as air pollution is illustrated by the case of Roger Diamond, a California lawyer who quixotically filed a $500 billion suit against 291 corporations, charging them with responsibility for the air pollution problem in his state. The $500 billion figure was based on the alleged effects of smog on "health, comfort, and welfare."[210] These effects might be presumed to include agricultural losses, property damages, moving expenses (for people forced out of the state), medical bills, cleaning bills, salaries of pollution control employees, and time spent by legislators.

All of these can be expressed in dollars. But what about millions of painful chests or reddened eyes? What about a discouraged community? If there is no medical bill, is there no loss? If there are no spiritual bills to pay, are there no spiritual costs? Some economists may be tempted to equate the cost of irritation to the price people are willing to pay to remove it. Unfortunately, things are not quite that neat.[211] People do not always react to the stresses of life as they do to the calls of an auctioneer. Those who are depressed by the ugliness of a city do not necessarily want to pay *any-thing* to change it. They may, in fact, be quite unaware that an unpolluted city is any better than a polluted one. Perhaps, if everybody in Los Angeles woke up one morning and the air were completely clean, the cars and buildings clean, the vistas crystal clear, and the orchids and violets blooming, they would suddenly realize how much the difference is worth and be willing to pay. Unfortunately, the policy is still pay first, taste later. But if an individual doesn't care one way or the other, if he has managed to get along in a clouded environment and is not particularly inclined to pay to change it, does this mean that there has been no cost to him?

Perhaps it distorts the meaning of cost to argue otherwise. Yet it may be that one of the greatest impacts of cars on people has been to deprive them of any feel for what it would be like to be in closer touch both with other people and the environment. Certainly, dull cities have dulled our sensitivities to the pleasure of breathing fresh air. The omnipresent smell of exhaust has taught us to keep our noses closed. The noise of engines and horns has forced us to "tune out" noise. Commuters become accustomed to congestion, and many children regard it as a fact of life that baseball players too young for Little League must share their play-streets with cars. Riding in cars wherever we go, we forget (or never learn) how satisfying it can be to ride bicycles, or walk, or even run. Ironically, it may be the lack of desire to pay, rather than the desire, which is one of the principal indicators of the social cost of cars. It is no wonder that Roger Diamond's suit was dismissed by a Superior Court judge on the grounds that the problem was "much too complex for a court to handle."[212]

The dulling of public sensitivities by omnipresent fumes, noises, dangers, and frustrations does not reflect conscious planning by the auto establishment, although it has in some ways worked in their favor by reducing the desire for an alternative system. The makers are not "robber barons," despite their proclivity for twisting both arms and meanings. Nor are their factories "dark, satanic mills," despite the horrors they have imposed on America.[213] But the makers are not angels either. They are worried about this business of social costs, which has been sneaking up on them for years and now haunts them like a reprimand from the past. They are not quite sure what they have done to the country, and they do not want to be found guilty of having hurt it.

It is not surprising, in view of the makers' desire to neatly justify their behavior, and in view of their persistent desire to explain all things in dollars, that they have begun to talk about social costs as if they are simply a part of the overhead. According to this view, the increased cost of being responsible must be passed on to the customer, as would any normal cost of production. The injustice of this view is that it assumes that the impending costs are normal, when actually they are emergency measures. Detroit's asking the public to pay for drastic measures now is like a doctor expecting a patient to pay for an operation which was necessitated by the doctor's own mistakes. It is a testimony to the crassness of Detroit's executives

that they should want to "sell" the public something they have been, in effect, stealing from the
public all these years, its health and its freedom.
These things are the public's by right, and they
should be restored as quickly as possible, regardless
of the cost to the industry.

President Nixon's science adviser, Lee DuBridge,
said in 1969 that he thought consumers had reached
the point where they were "willing to pay" the costs
of keeping technology under control.[214] But the fact
that someone is willing to pay for the preservation
of his life—or the restoration of ecological balance—hardly proves he should have to do so. The
payment of ransom doesn't justify the practice of
kidnapping, although it may encourage it. The auto
industry has been much encouraged by the profit
potential of pollution devices as a substitute for
real innovation, and it has been encouraged by
DuBridge's pronouncements that the internal
combustion engine is here to stay, at least until
the 1980s or 1990s.[215] DuBridge's forecasting efforts
are flatly contradicted, however, by those of dozens
of experts who testified in Senate hearings, and his
judgment about social costs is flatly contradicted
by many economists. One of these is Neil H. Jacoby,
a conservative member of the Council of Economic
Advisers in the Eisenhower Administration, who
said in 1969 that he thought the auto industry
"should be made to bear such costs as highway
policing and extra-high auto insurance premiums."[216]

To some extent, of course, the public shares the responsibility for the misdirection of the car and should share the burden of setting it straight. Mistakes which are the unforeseen results of worthy objectives are quite different from those which are the result of industrial greed. This book emphasizes those things which seem "bad" in the world of cars, but it should be acknowledged that much of this bad is, ironically, only a distortion of something which started out to be very good. The invention of the assembly line made it possible to increase by an enormous factor the mobility (and hence freedom) of the American people. At the same time, it made possible the reduplication of every lethal defect in design—and the dehumanization of work—by an equally large factor. Similarly, while cars enhance the freedom of those who have them, they increase the isolation of those who don't (in many suburban areas, one is literally stranded without a car). And while roads have become the lifelines that enable the suburbs to drift away from the cities, they have also become the noose on which the central business districts of the cities have slowly strangled. It is an extreme irony that the institution whose great contribution to civilization is its capacity to speed the circulation of people and goods from place to place, should become the instrument of a congestion so crippling that the civilization's major centers are dying from (among other things) a *lack* of circulation. It is just as ironic that an institution which may give individual Americans more sense of self-control than anything else their technology has invented should also be an instrument rivaling war itself as a means of self-destruction.

Thomas Jefferson said, "It is not by the consolidation, or centralization of powers, but by their distribution, that good government is effected." What is true of good government must now be true of big business, and particularly the automobile business. Richard Goodwin says the most sensitive nerve in the American consciousness is the individual's desire for mastery over his own life. The concentration of power in the automobile industry has destroyed this mastery in more ways than one.

First, cars have been used by their makers, advertently and inadvertently, as a cultural anesthetic. Not only because their omnipresence has deadened physical and kinesthetic sensitivities, but also because in spite of all the millions of different combinations of models, options, and colors available to "discriminating" car buyers, most American cars are aesthetically indistinguishable. When Barry Goldwater said in 1964 that what America needs is a "choice, not an echo," he might well have been speaking of cars. When George Wallace said in 1968 that there's not a "dime's worth of difference," he could easily have been speaking of Cadillacs and Fords. The offerings of Detroit are a perennial insult to the individuality of its customers, who are given little more to choose from than a wide selection of gimmicks. Of course, there is nothing wrong with the policy of designing cars for mass consumption; the same thing happens with food, clothes, and most other commodities. The difference is that with food and clothes the consumer still has a choice. If he doesn't like to eat chopped steak and wear white shirts, he still has the freedom to make cous-cous and wear a robe. With Chevrolets, Fords, and Buicks, the choice is like the one provided by the mess-hall sergeant who growls: "Sure you gotta choice. You can have a little hash or a lotta hash." That bloated size and overbearing power should be the distinguishing characteristics of a man's car is a fact of life about which he has little to say. A driver's attitude toward other drivers, pedestrians, the natural environment, and even the diminishing resource of urban space, is implicitly—if not consciously—expressed by the kind of car he drives. That his car has been styled and promoted to bear the unwritten label "I am impudent and proud of it," is not for him to question. The Plymouth "Road Runner" is named after a vacuous cartoon character whose principal distinction is that he always succeeds in "putting down" his rivals. Mustangs and Cobras are built with their rear ends conspicuously raised in defiance of whoever follows behind. Mercuries and Cadillacs put their defiance up front, with noses thrust forward like the business end of a torpedo. If it happens to be against a person's grain to be flashy, sharp, rude, defensive, and cool, he is simply not going to feel comfortable riding around in a torpedo. If what he values is economy, reliability, and practicality in his car—along with a body design which offers both congeniality to its occupants and a reasonable lack of hostility toward strangers outside—he is offered nothing by Detroit. The Maverick, widely advertised as a "practical" car, is a foolish compromise, looking more like a slightly scaled-down version of the usual absurdity than a useful compartment for people and goods. If Volkswagens were not available from abroad, many Americans would find themselves as much ignored by the bogus "supply and demand" of the automobile market as hungry Negroes were ignored by the supply and demand for restaurant service in the pre-1964 South. It is the makers' policy of planned psychological obsolescence, of course, which forces designers to resort to gimmicks and grotesqueries in order to come up with something "new" each year. Since World War II, these fruits of the stylists' labor have become the distinguishing marks of the American landscape.

Second, the car as an institution creates a crippling dependency. Quite aside from the demand created by obsolescent styles, people seem to want more and more cars and seem more and more unable to function without them. Whereas Europeans get along with one car for each ten people, Americans now have one six-passenger car for every *two* people, even though only one of those two people is likely to be driving at any given moment.

Business, of course, would clank to a complete
halt without motor vehicles. But the general public
is equally dependent. The car is a fragile lifeboat
of suburban survival. Psychologically, the suburbs
(which cars made possible) ara often lonely and
remote; the resident yearns for a life which requires
much more than just houses and streets. As Goodwin puts it, "At home, he, can either sit amid his
many purchases or get back into his car and drive
to visit friends."[217] Physically, he is isolated because
no other form of transportation is available. He
hasn't ridden a bicycle for years and would feel
undignified on a scooter. Mass transit has never
been given a chance, and distances are too far for
walking. Besides, in many suburbs (such as those
in Montgomery County, Maryland, just outside of
Washington, D.C.) there are no sidewalks. Children
must either walk in the street or be driven to school.
Naturally, they are driven and the car-dependency
is reinforced. When these suburbs finally get
around to building sidewalks—probably as a deco-
rative reminder of an earlier age, like gas street-
lamps and iron hitching posts—the children will
doubtless refuse to walk on them.

Finally, the car culture is an insatiable consumer
of time, the most finite resource available to any
human being, not only time spent directly, but time
spent earning money to buy and maintain it. In
terms of money alone, the car is a staggering burden. To the average citizen, a new car consumes
the entire income from seven months of work. That

doesn't include the costs of depreciation, gas, oil, servicing, repairs, insurance, garaging, parking, tolls, new tires, accessories, registration, titling, and three or four kinds of taxes. In 1964, according to a study by the Bureau of Public Roads, these costs amounted to $10,162 for the life of each car, or well over $1,000 a year.[218]

Since then, however, things have grown much worse. In 1970, many city-dwellers and commuters were paying far more for parking than the decreased buying power of the dollar would explain. In New York, for example, rates in some lots had reached $80 and $90 per month by 1969, and additional rate increases were being filed with the city at a rate of 100 to 150 a month.[219] These rates, of course, do not include the cost of damage caused by parking cars too close together. Nor do they include the wear to the engine sustained by attendants gunning cold cars up and down steep ramps. For the urban dweller, therefore, parking *alone* may amount to as much as $1000 a year (as contrasted to the Bureau of Public Roads' 1964 figure of $188 for both parking and tolls.)

For those who decide to park on the street, there are other problems, some of them costly enough to nullify any advantage of getting a free space. In New York, residents have to jump out of bed at odd hours to move cars from one side of the street to the other in compliance with alternate-day parking regulations. Cars which aren't moved are either ticketed or towed away at the owner's expense. In Washington, the law permits no parking within forty feet of any intersection. Total enforcement would reduce parking capacity by as many as sixteen cars per intersection and by thousands of cars per day. The law is therefore enforced only partially, causing thousands of drivers to gamble on not getting tickets. The long-term result is that most drivers get just enough tickets so that it doesn't really matter whether they are renting a space or not. Any remaining saving in cash is effectively wiped out by the higher incidence of vandalism (in some areas, antenna-snapping seems to be a favorite sport), sideswiping (cars without running boards don't have a chance on today's streets), theft (usually involving a broken vent as well as a loss of property), and general deterioration from constant exposure to rain, soot, salt, and polluted air.

The costs of insurance have inflated just as rapidly. Between 1967 and 1969, accident claims increased 40 percent, and rates rose accordingly. Nationwide Mutual announced that rates for high-powered cars would be increased 50 percent, beginning in 1970. "Then the vast majority of owners who drive standard-powered cars will be relieved of the burden of subsidizing the higher losses of high-powered vehicles," promised a Nationwide representative.[220] But instead of lowering its rates for most owners, Nationwide quietly *raised* them several months later.

As with parking, however, the costs of insurance

are far greater for certain categories of people. Particularly unfortunate are the old, the young, the unmarried, those who are members of certain racial or occupational categories, and, above all, those who have had accidents. Even accidents which are not the driver's fault cause rates to rise painfully, and some drivers feel constrained to hide news of all but the severest accidents from their insurance companies. Yet the average car is involved in two accidents in its lifetime, and the average driver's chances of avoiding an accident for more than five years are very tenuous.

The irony of auto insurance is that it insures people only as long as they prove impervious to accident. Insurance companies have become more and more fickle about who they won't cover and why. The costs, both to those who are covered and those who aren't, continue to rise. In one recent year, rates were increased in forty-five states. At the same time, thousands of motorists were mysteriously dropped (many had never had accidents), and thousands more were refused coverage for reasons incomprehensible to anyone who was outside the industry. Investigations of such "arbitrary underwriting" were not long in coming, and it was quickly established that major companies had issued warnings to their agents to avoid selling insurance to categories of people considered "undesirable." Undesirability was not defined, but even cursory review of these warnings suggests that the criteria are highly subjective. Included in the "bad risk" lists are such groups as professional athletes, musicians, entertainers, waiters, janitors, porters, busboys, parking lot attendants, bellhops, and the like. Faced with accusations of racial and geographic discrimination, insurance companies hastily pointed out that cars which are kept on the street in the inner city are subject to a higher incidence of vandalism and theft. The implication is that the companies cannot insure inner city drivers without losing money. Such explanations, however, do not "explain" the many cases in which drivers were dropped because their own behavior (other than driving behavior) was deemed unacceptable by the company. For example, one man had his policy canceled because he allegedly had a "filthy house."[221]

Recent investigations of the auto insurance industry have put the companies' laments in a new light. The argument that auto insurance is unprofitable, it seems, is based on a method of accounting that very cleverly fails to tell the whole story. Insurance companies invest the money they take in from sales of premiums, and while they may in fact lose money on the sales, the investment income produces an overall profit that more than compensates for any losses. In reporting their financial condition to the public (and to the agencies which decide whether or not to let them raise their rates), they do not mention any investment income. In view of this practice, discrimination against policyholders or would-be policyholders may represent more of an effort to make the rich richer at the expense of the poor than an effort to stay financially afloat.[222]

There is at least one way in which costs could be reduced for both the insurance companies and their customers, however. While it is hard to reduce the number of accidents, it may be quite easy to reduce the costs of those which occur. Cars which have been damaged in collisions are expensive to repair because they are not *designed* to be repaired. Many replacement items would be inexpensive except for unnecessary inaccessibility, and in some cases labor is ten times the cost of the item involved. Other items, apparently, are not made to be replaced or repaired at all. As one expert told a group of body engineers, "I don't know of any tool available in the repair field which will make square or oval holes in metal panels, yet new exterior ornamentation requires such holes. Imagine what a body man has to say about you when he has to use a file to square out a drilled hole. . ." Of course, the body man collects ample compensation for his labor. And the insurance companies collect whatever premiums are necessary to cover the expense of repairing cars which are styled to look good *before* they have their first accidents. As usual, it is the customer who foots the bill when the accident finally happens.

The Bureau of Public Roads grossly underestimates the dollar cost of cars for many Americans—and probably for all Americans. For millions, the annual direct and indirect dollar cost now amounts to $2000 or $3000 per year, a whopping proportion of the average family income.

On top of the time spent earning all this money, there is the time spent directly on, in, under, with, or around the car.[223] Rush-hour drivers often spend two hours per day crawling a short but painfully slow distance to work and back. Moviegoers often spend all of the short and ten minutes of the feature looking for a place to leave their albatrosses. On winter days, when garden hoses are frozen, suburbanites will spend half a Saturday afternoon waiting in line for a two minute car-wash at the local shopping center. And then, of course, there is servicing. Getting to a repair shop and back within the course of a single day is no mean trick, as Russell Baker has observed in the *New York Times:* "The ideal car, as opposed to a dreamboat, would come equipped with a repair shop in the next block. Instead, practically all places of automobile repair are now being moved progressively farther from the places where car owners live, collide, and weep for dynamic obsolescence.

"The typical repair shop nowadays is located at a place which has six digits in its address. A typical repair shop street number is 973456 Beltway Plaza." Baker correctly notes that modern America has forgotten all about the problem of getting to work (or wherever) once we have left the car at the shop. If visits to the shop were no more frequent than visits to the hospital, this might not be a problem, but to some owners, the repair shop is agonizingly familiar. "As a car starts to age, even if it is not parked vigorously against large oaks, the occasions on which it must be taken to the shop increase with alarming frequency. Whole weeks are chalked up in each year simply getting the engine tuned, the headlights aligned, the brakes tightened, the hoses replaced, the wipers repaired, the carburetor adjusted, the muffler replaced." Baker concludes by comparing the ownership of a car, or "dream-boat," to the punishment of Sisyphus, who was condemned by the gods to spend eternity rolling a boulder up a hill.[224]

But Russell Baker is not the first to make such observations about the American proclivity for self-punishment. Just before the automobile was invented, in a discussion of the peculiar "economy" of American life, Henry David Thoreau observed that we spend most of our lives laboriously pushing our barns down the road.[225] His point was that the work a man does often becomes, even in its most tedious and enervating forms, an end in itself rather than a means of enabling him to reach beyond himself. The potential value of the automobile, it might be conjectured, is that it can *free* men to live better lives—by saving time, by increasing experience, and by extending the scope of their world. For most of us, that value has never been realized. Instead, we break our bodies bringing food to a dinosaur. Through helplessness or ignorance, we keep the auto makers' oligopoly thriving by faithfully catering to its unnatural appetites. Instead of being freed by the car, we have been trapped by it, obliged to spend half of our working lives earning money to maintain it, forced to inhale its obnoxious and debilitating fumes, surrounded by its roads on all sides, and even seduced by its makers into believing that we are getting a remarkable bargain in the bargain. Instead of being carried along the road of progress by our cars, we—to paraphrase Thoreau—spend much of our lives pushing our cars ahead of us.

Lest it be too quickly concluded that the automobile in America has come to no good, it should be clearly noted that all this has been rather good for GM. And there may be those who can find comfort in the words of former GM president Charles ("Engine Charlie") Wilson, who said, *"What's good for GM is good for the U.S."*

VII—WHAT'S EVEN BETTER

If there is anything more dangerous than a leader with reckless courage, it is a leader with no courage at all. What is true of individuals is also true of institutions, particularly those institutions upon whose leadership the course of the future depends.

General Motors Corporation is such an institution. The decisions it makes are not merely matters of detail within broad policies set by other institutions. GM is a maker of policy at the broadest level. Its actions determine some of the most fundamental directions of society. Yet GM poses a grave danger to society because as a corporate body it is crippled by an appalling fear—of risk, of new challenges to its old economic and moral assumptions, and of the very future it has been entrusted with helping to build.

A few hours before GM's annual meeting in May 1970, Robert Townsend, a former Avis executive and author of the bestselling *Up the Organization,* told a group of shareholders: "Jim Roche is really a very nice guy, only he stopped thinking and lost all his guts thirty years ago." It is highly significant that in the GM organization the chairman is virtually an extension of the corporation itself. If GM were not severely lacking in the qualities of leadership required of America's most important institutions in an age of almost kaleidoscopic change, it would have chosen a different breed of chairman years ago.

No less than the Daughters of the American Revolution or the U.S. House of Representatives, the far-flung empire of General Motors is suffering from a case of acute gerontacracy—and all of America is suffering as a result. In the most mobile society on earth, the basic transportation system lies in the hands of a senile and witless giant. There are, no doubt, thousands of auto industry employees for whom the events described in this book are genuinely embarrassing. Many of the workers on the line, for example, do not endorse their management's reactionary attitudes toward new technology. But the GM complex is so vast, and its patterns so rigid, that the attitudes of dissident individuals count for little. While some of the more sensitive employees recognize that the world really *is* different from the golden age of the 1950s, the organization as a whole continues to act as if nothing has changed—and as if the environmental "scare" were nothing more than a passing whim of the public.

Thus, in May 1970, GM spent hundreds of thousands of dollars preparing films, brochures, and letters to convince its shareholders that the worst of the scare is now over. But the worst is far from over. In the last week of July 1970, the east coast of the United States was plunged into its most putrid smog since the invention of the automobile—a smog so threatening to the lives of city dwellers that New York's Mayor John Lindsay announced a severe curtailing of automobile traffic, and hinted that cars might eventually have to be banned from the city altogether.

It is now clear that we cannot afford to depend on the stricken social consciences of auto executives to change the self-indulgent habits of the industry. It is equally clear that only when the economic structure of the auto industry is radically reformed will our troubles with cars begin to abate. If the Justice Department under President Johnson had proceeded with its plan to restore competition to the industry by divesting GM of its monopolistic grip on the market, we might all be breathing easier today. Instead, the cloud of smog which now pursues us like the ghost of our future is accompanied by a worsening of costs on all fronts. President Johnson, it is said, aborted the antitrust suit because of its potential political cost. Presumably, it is a similar sense of political parsimony which has convinced President Nixon and Attorney-General John Mitchell to keep *their* hands off.

So if James Roche happens to be burdened with a shortage of courage and far-sightedness, he is no more guilty of failing to make GM responsible than are the leaders of many other segments of society, from the president, who refuses to risk raising the ire of big business for the sake of his countrymen's lungs and limbs, to the commuter who refuses to give up the phallic gratification of riding two miles to work in an eighteen-foot torpedo rather than suffer the inconvenience of taking a bus, or riding a bicycle, or even trying out the sagging muscles of his own neglected calves.

Five years ago, it might have been oddly romantic to suggest that Americans should have to suffer inconveniences of any kind. And it would have seemed laughably un-hip to speak of the need to have "guts" in a world where the highest paid men (Roche's $650,000 salary makes him the highest paid executive in the nation) are those who fit most smoothly into the systems of which they themselves are the perfect products. But inconvenience may be the only alternative to the fatal comfort of continuing to do what we are doing now. As French poet Pierre Emanuel said before a symposium on the impact of technology on culture, "America is prophetic of the tension of the modern age and will have to suffer through it. America will help humanity to rediscover the meaning and necessity of suffering in a world of change."

The changes that must now take place in General Motors and the rest of the automotive establishment will not be easy to accomplish; yet the hardships will be more psychological and social than economic. Mental sets, physical habits, and rigid social patterns will pose heavy resistance to the demands of the future. The responsibility for recognizing these demands and breaking through the resistance rests on all Americans, but particularly on those who have had the power to act all along, but who have failed to do so.

• In the Department of Justice, the time has come to blow the dust off the suit to divest GM of its giant Chevrolet Division. GM's market control clearly violates the intention of antitrust law, as Justice's lawyers well knew when they began preparing their case. Mitchell's support of legislation permitting police to enter private homes without knocking, contrasted with his unwillingness to interfere with operations of mammoth corporations whose negligent policies contribute to more needless dying than all criminals, addicts, and militant revolutionaries in America, is a mockery of the Justice Department.

• Another agency which has done little more than collect stale air in its GM file is the Federal Trade Commission, which is no exception to the rule that Americans are having difficulties getting their priorities straight. Clearly, this is an agency in which the first priority should be to eliminate the grossest violations of trade regulations which have come to its attention. The FTC has long been cognizant of the effects of Detroit's oligopoly on the pocketbook of the American consumer. Yet it has taken no significant action to remedy a steadily deteriorating situation. Instead, it has been content to save its criticisms for lesser (and less threatening) industries. In 1970, for example, the FTC began an investigation of the three major makers of breakfast cereals to determine whether their advertising and control over the industry is resulting in higher consumer prices. According to David

Vienna of the *Washington Post,* "This investigation breaks new ground in federal antitrust work by focusing attention on whether a few companies can so dominate an industry that they in effect act as monopolists. This is the first major investigation under an economic theory that four companies can act as a monopoly if they control more than 50 percent of a market."

FTC economists suspect that the "Big Three" of American breakfast foods—Kellogg, General Foods, and General Mills—are controlling the cereal market through heavy advertising. They argue that a corn flake is a corn flake no matter who makes it, and that the manufacturers depend on voluminous advertising to "differentiate" one product from another. The cost of this advertising is passed on to the consumer, who simply pays a little more for his breakfast. It also helps to perpetuate the oligopoly of the three major cereal makers by preventing new companies, which can't afford such heavy advertising, from entering the market on a competitive basis. If the FTC decides to act, it will be either to seek divestiture of some products or to limit advertising by the "Big Three."

Now, for those who always *said* there wasn't any difference between Post Toasties and Kellogg's Corn Flakes, the FTC's concern may come as welcome news. But what about the man who could never see much difference between a Chevy and a Ford? Is he going to be asked to keep right on subsidizing the millions of dollars of advertising the

Big Three spend to differentiate products which on their own merits are often as indistinguishable as corn flakes? Is he going to be asked to pay the cost of keeping new companies out of the auto manufacturing business so that the existing companies can charge him higher prices for products he has no choice but to buy from them? Certainly, if the FTC is serious about the theory of the four-company monopoly, it must be painfully serious about Detroit. For while the Big Three of breakfast food control 80% of their market, the Big Three of automobiles control a much greater percentage of a far greater market. If the FTC is willing to take on the corn flakes industry, it must be equally willing to take on the *real* Big Three. If limiting advertising would restore healthy competition to Battle Creek, it would have a double benefit for Detroit. In addition to lowering the obstacles to new companies, it could free enormous sums of money for such useful enterprises as pollution control and highway safety research.

• In the Department of Transportation, news of America's problems with cars has apparently not yet been received. Yet, this department bears a vital responsibility. If it is essential that intercompany competition be restored to the auto industry, it is at least equally essential that *intermode* competition be restored to the transportation industry as a whole. The DOT is not completely responsible for the inexplicable neglect (and inevitable killing off) of alternatives to the private automobile, but it has certainly done its part to hasten the process. It is desperately important that Secretary John Volpe do everything in his power to bring about the replacement of the highway trust fund with a *transportation* fund, out of which a sane and balanced transportation program can be funded for the first time. Volpe's speeches have often revealed his awareness that mass transit must be given a great boost if American cities are to survive. But Volpe will have to show considerably more courage than he has shown so far, and even then he cannot succeed without the help of certain congressmen (such as Rep. John C. Kluczynski, chairman of the Roads Subcommittee) who are not likely to want to jeopardize their profitable relationships with the trucking lobby.

• In Congress, responsibilities are more scattered. As long as the auto industry proves incapable of disciplining itself, Congress will have to employ a variety of stick-and-carrot schemes to control it. Unfortunately, it is often as not the auto industry, rather than Congress, which wields the stick and dangles the carrot. Still, there are enough farsighted senators and representatives in Washington to raise hopes that legislation can be used to effect major changes both in the auto industry and in the industry's relationships to other segments of society. Most needed is an incentive for the commercial production of an inherently nonpolluting automobile engine. The best bet is for the federal government to stimulate the production of nonpolluting engines by changing the procurement policies for its own vehicles. At the same time, Congress should waste no time authorizing the DOT to make outright grants to private individuals or organizations for the development of alternatives to the internal combustion engine. Another possibility is to place a graduated pollution tax on all motor vehicles, such that engines which fail to equal the standard of the cleanest feasible engine are so severely penalized that their production is quickly abandoned. Similar tax penalties could be used to encourage the use of high-impact bumpers as standard equipment; to force manufacturers to take both repair and disposal problems into consideration in the design of new vehicles; and to encourage recycling of junk cars and scrap tires by both manufacturers and consumers.

The possibilities are endless, and there is no point in cataloguing them here. If effective incentives do not now exist, it is not because there haven't been plenty of solid proposals; nor is it because the ideas proposed have been technologically or economically unfeasible. The files of federal agencies are well stuffed with studies showing step-by-step strategies for putting such proposals to work. It remains to be seen whether Congress has enough vision to do anything more than shuffle a few papers and wait for the auto issue to die.

• While the federal government worries about funds and feasibility, state and local governments will have to prepare for real physical changes. It is only a matter of time before cars are banned in downtown sections of major cities, and the sooner the better. Mayor Lindsay has shown courage in asserting that for his own city this is the only way to escape the automobile-highway chokehold. New York is not unique, but it will probably have to set an example for smaller, more conservative municipalities. Left to their own devices, there are many cities which will smother in their own effluence before they will act. Yet for all the responsibility carried by the federal government, some of the most crucial decisions can only be made at the local level. It is the local residents and merchants who must decide to tear up their streets and make heavy investments in new subways or moving sidewalks. It is they who must turn their backs on the seductive offers of the highway establishment to give nine fat dollars for every dollar of their own they are willing to spend on you know what.

Obviously, there will be risks to any city which undertakes such changes. No one can be sure what the final effect will be. But greater risks are assumed by Americans everyday in Southeast Asia, for reasons which are far less clear. If zeal is warranted in defending the country against its enemies, then zeal is warranted in the building of demonstration projects for the defense of dying cities. There will be bitter battle with those whose interests are tied to the past, and for this reason much of the ammunition will have to come from those whose only hope lies in the future. The urban poor, whose houses are always the first to be torn up for new freeways built mainly for middle-class suburbanites, and whose imprisonment makes them least able to escape the debilitating effects of the overladen air, will be among the leaders of the movement.

It takes little vision, however, to see that the poor are not the only ones who are imprisoned. The atmosphere of the earth envelopes us all, and the poison within it is spreading rapidly. There is no possibility of escaping its effects by keeping the car windows closed and the air-conditioning on. Even such isolated citizens as David Rockefeller, Chairman of the Board of the Chase Manhattan Bank (whose insistence on being chauffeured by private limousine to the doorstep of his Wall Street office each morning may prove to be a major impediment to the development of a more benificent transit system in Lower Manhattan) will have to recognize sooner or later that in this world we are all members of the same family.

As another Rockefeller—John D. ("Jay") IV—said on the occasion of GM's 1970 meeting, efforts to bring about major reforms in American transportation are a "logical outgrowth of something very good that is happening in this country—an increasing demand for accountability and participation."

• The only way to improve the accountability of GM is to assure the participation of everyone else. The saying that "everyone owns a little GM" is hyperbolic, but significant. "One individual shareholder is part of the decision making process," says Jay Rockefeller, "but for the most part in America, he doesn't know that. I see that as one of the major contributions Campaign GM will have—to bring that small shareholder into a position of demanding accountability." For both institutional shareholders (banks, churches, universities, etc.) and individuals, this means recognizing that it is not necessarily the solemn duty of a loyal shareholder to vote his shares the way GM's management says he should simply because "management knows best."

It is now clear that there are many companies—and GM is a prime example—in which the management knows pitifully little about what policies are "best." GM's directors represent an extremely narrow sector, demographically speaking, of the shareholder population at large. None of these directors have been black, female, poor, or young. None have been elected to the board by democratic process, although the machinery of democracy has been part of the corporate structure all along. Every GM director is elected to his seat by a process which makes the same mockery of the individual shareholder's "vote" as a Russian election. The candidates are chosen by management and presented to the shareholders for their approval.

Candidates nominated by dissident shareholders

have had no chance to win, simply because the vast majority of the owners of GM's 280 million shares comprise a silent, anonymous and apparently uncaring group of people who either never vote or vote automatically in favor of management's wishes. Yet these are the people on whose reluctant shoulders GM's responsibilities to society must finally settle. If the annual elections for GM's board are a sham, it is up to the shareholders—particularly the institutional shareholders who have a good deal of influence of their own—to expose it. If the sham persists (which is quite likely), concerned shareholders will have to find ways to circumvent the election process altogether.

One way or another, the industry's leaders will have to be rendered responsive to the fact that they can no longer simply hand out profits without providing a thorough, uncooked accounting of the financial and social costs which made these profits possible. In the absence of honest communication between the auto companies and their shareholders, there can be no approach to the day when the things that are "good for GM" really *are* good for the United States.

NOTES

1. *Automobile Facts and Figures,* Automobile Manufacturers Association (Detroit, 1969), p. 18.

2. Robert Ayres and Allen Kneese, Resources for the Future, Inc., Washington, D.C., 1969.

3. United States Department of Transportation, Bureau of Public Roads, Tables W-201 and VM-1, cited in *Automobile Facts and Figures,* p. 51.

4. *Automobile Facts and Figures,* p. 38. A "long" trip is any trip which involves "household members being out of town at least overnight or going on a one-day trip to a place 100 miles from home."

5. Bicycles, buses, carveyors, helicopters, hovercraft, maxi-taxis, motorcycles, moving sidewalks, monorails, planes, trains, trolleys, subways, *and walking.* None of these alternatives does everything a car can do; but each can do things cars *can't* do. No one mode, not even cars, has a monopoly on the attributes of good transportation.

6. The four corporations are American Motors, Chrysler, Ford, and General Motors; the dominant member of the group is General Motors, which is larger than the other three combined (see Chapter 3).

7. J. D. Braman, Assistant Secretary for Urban Systems and Environment, United States Department of Transportation, said in a speech before the Western Regional Conference of the American Transit Association on June 9, 1969: "T. S. Eliot, poet and critic, once said that he foresaw the end of the world as happening not with a bang but with a whimper. There is a growing body of opinion that he may have been right and that the first stage of the final crisis is already upon us—that the dying whimper of an environment burdened to the point of collapse may come before another fifty years has passed."

8. A 1969 poll of American adults in 138 cities, conducted

by a Princeton, N.J., research team, found that 62 percent of the respondents were in favor of outlawing the sale of internal combustion engines by 1975, while only 23 percent opposed the idea.

9. A forty-foot-tall "monument to the American dream," the principal exhibit at the 1968 meeting of the International Design Conference in April, consisted of thirty junked automobiles in a heap, painted white.

10. Private interview as reported in International Research and Technology IDEAS (Information on Developments in Electricity and Steam) Washington, December 1969.

11. An Oliphant cartoon published in 1969 (Los Angeles *Times Syndicate)* depicts a bewildered citizen sinking slowly into a morass of filth, holding aloft a sign reading "POLLUTION LATEST: SCIENCE SEES END OF LIFE ON EARTH IN 35 YEARS!" Watching from the shore is a fat industrialist with a relieved expression on his face. He is saying, "Boy, you had me worried for a moment there—I thought you said three to five years!" The industrialist is surrounded by belching smokestacks and spouting pipes. He is even contributing to the effluence with a thick cigar. *But nowhere is there a sign of a motor vehicle.*

12. "The Automobile and Air Pollution: A Program for Progress" (Part II), United States Department of Commerce (December 1967), pp. 2-4.

13. Donald E. Carr, *The Breath of Life* (New York: W. W. Norton & Company, Inc., 1965), p. 157.

14. "The Air Quality Act of 1967," pamphlet published by the United States Department of Health, Education and Welfare, n.d.

15. Carr, p. 63.

16. *Ibid.,* p. 58.

17. "Air Pollution—Present and Future," city of Livermore Air Pollution Control Study Committee, March 1968, cited in *The Search for a Low-Emission Vehicle,* staff report prepared by the Senate Commerce Committee, 1969, p. 3.

18. Robert U. Ayres, International Research and Tech-

nology Corporation, Washington, D.C., 1968.

19. "Motor Vehicle Safety Defect Recall Campaigns," reported to the National Highway Safety Bureau by domestic and foreign vehicle manufacturers, United States Department of Transportation, 1969.

20. Carr, p. 87.

21. *Air Conservation:* The Report of the Air Conservation Commission of the American Association for the Advancement of Science, Publication No. 80 (Washington: 1965), p. 91.

22. *The Search for a Low-Emission Vehicle,* Staff Report prepared for the Committee on Commerce, U.S. Senate, 1967, p. 1.

23. Reported by Stuart Auerbach in the *Washington Post,* November 11, 1969.

24. *Air Conservation,* p. 952.

25. *Ibid.,* p. 142. In addition, Carr observes: "The possibility of cancer from smog has been a great boon to the tobacco industry and its hard-pressed public relations people, because it gives them a somewhat precarious whipping boy." (p. 105)

26. Hearings before the Subcommittee on Air and Water Pollution of the Committee on Public Works, United States Senate, 90th Cong., 2nd sess., July 1968, p. 680.

27. Joseph M. Callahan, "Smog Battle Won, Industry Says: Meeting California Standards Called Final Round," *Automotive News,* May 26, 1969, p. 1.

28. Jerry M. Flint, *New York Times,* April 13, 1969, p. 25.

29. Barsky might have added that when driving wasn't hurting the control devices, the control devices were hurting driving. As noted in April 1968 *Consumer Reports,* "Although two years of experience with the problems caused by smog-control modification in California should have given manufacturers some valuable guidelines on maintaining engine performance, many of the new cars with such modifications turned out to be inexcusably hard to start and keep moving."

30. *The Search for a Low-Emission Vehicle,* pp. 5-6.

31. "Automobile Air Pollution Control Costs: Background Paper Prepared for the Interagency Pollution Control Incentive Study Committee by The Economic and Social Studies Section, Office of Legislative and Public Affairs, National Center for Air Pollution Control," March 20, 1968.

32. Opposing interests continued to quibble about weight-power ratios, relative complexity, fuel economy, public acceptance, etc. But there were no arguments about basic concepts.

33. Alden Self-Transit Systems Corporation, Westboro, Massachusetts; Alsat Industries, Detroit; American Motors Corporation, Detroit; Army Engineers R&D Laboratory, Fort Belvoir, Virginia; Battronic Truck Corporation, Boyertown, Pennsylvania; Chrysler Corporation, Detroit; ESB, Inc. (Formerly Electric Storage Battery) Philadelphia; Electric Fuel Propulsion Inc., Ferndale, Michigan; Ford Motor Company, Dearborn; General Electric R&D Center, Schenectady, New York; General Motors Corporation, Warren, Michigan; Gould-National Batteries, Inc., St. Paul, Minnesota; Gulton Industries Inc., Metuchen, New Jersey; Linear Alpha Inc., Evanston, Illinois; National Union Electric Corporation, Stamford, Connecticut; The Potomac Edison Company, Hagerstown, Maryland; Rowan Controller Corporation (Rowan Industries) Oceanport, New Jersey; Stelber Industries Inc., Elmhurst, New York; West Penn Power Company, Connellsville, Pennsylvania; Westinghouse Electric Corporation, Pittsburgh, Pennsylvania; Gar Wood, Miami; Yardney Electric Corporation, New York, New York.

34. Private interview, as reported in International Research and Technology IDEAS, March 1969, pp. 48-50.

35. Joint hearings before the Committee on Commerce and the Subcommittee on Air and Water Pollution of the Committee on Public Works, United States Senate, 90th Cong., 2nd sess. May 27 and 28, 1968.

36. *Fortune,* July 1967, p. 79.

37. A "Panel on Electrically Powered Vehicles," appointed by the Department of Commerce in 1967 and chaired by

M.I.T. Professor Richard Morse concluded in 1968 that no electric car was likely to solve the pollution problem before 1978 but that the auto industry had an unfulfilled responsibility to work on other alternatives.

38. An electric car produced by the Copper Development Association had to carry 1700 lbs. of batteries.

39. International Research and Technology IDEAS, December 1969, p. 116.

40. Netchert, "The Economic Impact of Electric Vehicles," paper delivered before the International Electric Vehicle Symposium in Phoenix, Arizona, November 5, 1969.

41. The U.S. Forest Service says that tree fatalities caused by automobile pollution have become a major problem in some national forests.

42. *The Search for a Low-Emission Vehicle,* pp. 11-12.

43. *Ibid.,* p. 11.

44. Private letter.

45. *The Search for a Low-Emission Vehicle.*

46. A. Rothenberg, "Informal Visit with Henry Ford," *Look,* May 28, 1968, pp. 92-96.

47. "Future of the Automobile," *U.S. News and World Report,* February 10, 1969, p. 70.

48. Joseph Callahan, "Gaseous Fuels Cut Smog But Hope for Use is Slim," *Automotive News,* November 24, 1969, p. 20.

49. *Ibid.*

50. Editorial, *Automotive News,* November 24, 1969, p. 12.

51. Joint Hearings, "The Automobile Steam Engine and Other External Combustion Engine Alternatives to the Internal Combustion Engine," p. 160.

52. *Ibid.,* pp. 160-161.

53. "GM Progress of Power," exposition at General Motors Technical Center, Warren, Michigan, May 7, 1969.

54. Callahan, "GM Unveils Vast Research Efforts," *Automotive News,* May 12, 1969.

55. Hearings before the Subcommittee on Retailing, Distribution, and Marketing Practices and Subcommittee on Monopoly of the Select Committee on Small Business, United

States Senate, on "Planning, Regulation and Competition: Automobile Industry—1968," p. 965.

56. *Washington Post,* November 13, 1969, cited in International Research and Technology IDEAS, November 1969, p. 109.

57. International Research and Technology IDEAS, November 1969, p. 109.

58. *Ibid.,* January 1970, p. 3.

59. *Ibid.,* p. 6.

60. Irwin Hersey, "We Will Have to Run Very Hard Just to Stay Even . . .", *Engineering Opportunities,* May 1969.

61. Peter Bernstein, "Pollution Laws May Force End of Gasoline Car," *St. Louis Globe-Democrat,* July 13, 1969, p. 16A.

62. International Research and. Technology IDEAS, October 1969, p. 103.

63. *Ibid.,* December 1969, p. 116.

64. *Ibid.,* p. 115.

65. *Ibid.,* January 1970, p. 6.

66. *Ibid.,* p. 5.

67. *Automotive News,* December 22, 1969, p. 1.

68. Edward Ayres, "The Economic Impact of Conversion to a Nonpolluting Automobile," prepared for the Office of the Secretary, United States Department of Transportation, under contract PS-01040 to International Research and Technology, Washington, D.C., December 30, 1969.

69. We do not mean to imply that the steam car is God's answer to man's problems with cars. In the first place, American technology is far too versatile to justify the manifest destiny of any particular mode of propulsion. In the second place, the troubles caused by cars do not end with pollution. Later chapters point to a host of other afflictions, both physical and social. The struggle of the steam car is cited here only as an illustration of the difficulty *any* cure for automotive blight seems to have when it comes to gaining the cooperation it deserves from Detroit.

70. *Bulletin of the Atomic Scientists,* May 1969.

71. In an interesting review of the demise of the Corvair,

Robert Cumberford theorized that the real cause was not Ralph Nader's criticism, but GM's inability to go out on a limb and change the car, due to the company's vast, inflexible structure: "You must remember that GM is in effect a nation-state in itself, complete with Byzantine intrigues, political parties, militant factions, great lords and great rebels. Power within the corporation shifts constantly, without public knowledge, and the corporate equivalents of blood feuds do exist, as does the code of *omerata*. Men may nurture ideas for years, even for decades, before they are able to implement them." ("R.I.P. Corvair, 1960-1969," *Car and Driver,* August, 1969.)

72. "The Massive Statistics of General Motors," *Fortune,* July 15, 1966.

73. James M. Roche, Chairman of the Board and Chief Executive Officer of General Motors, at General Motors News Conference, Detroit, February 13, 1968.

74. Hearings on Planning, Regulation, and Competition, 1968, p. 102.

75. Roche, speech at Annual Mayor's Prayer Breakfast, Chicago, May 2, 1968.

76. Roche, speech at Dayton Golden Moments Dinner, National Cash Register Company, September 12, 1968.

77. Roche, "Understanding: The Key to Business-Government Cooperation," Illinois Manufacturers' Association, December 12, 1968.

78. Hearings on Planning, Regulation, and Competition, 1968, pp. 333, 547, 548.

79. Private interview, name withheld by request.

80. Hearings on Planning, Regulation, and Competition, 1968, pp. 546-548.

81. *Ibid.*

82. Hearings before the Federal Trade Commission on Automobile Pricing Practices, September 16, 1969.

83. Hearings on Planning, Regulation, and Competition, 1968.

84. *Ibid.,* pp. 20-23.

85. In any case, a judgment against GM amounts to closing

the barn door after the horse is out, since GM's stable of lawyers can always keep a suit in the courts until the issue is so dead (and perhaps the plaintiff too) that the outcome is a mere formality. One case against GMAC, for example, took fourteen years to decide. (Hearings before the Senate Subcommittee on Antitrust and Monopoly, Committee on the Judiciary, on Administered Prices, Part 6, Automobiles, 1958.)

86. Personal interview, December 1969.

87. Taylor, "Crisis in the Modern Economy."

88. Hearings on Planning, Regulation, and Competition, 1968, p. 391.

89. *Ibid.,* p. 919.

90. *Ibid.,* p. 212.

91. *Ibid.,* p. 1033.

92. Bob Irvin, "The Auto Industry: Competition Becomes a Merger When Smog Speech is Used," *Detroit News,* December 1, 1968.

93. Hearings on Planning, Regulation, and Competition, 1968, p. 961.

94. *Ibid.,* p. 242.

95. "The Automobile Industry: A Case Study of Competition" (A Statement by General Motors Corporation), October 18, 1968, p. 72.

96. Hearings on Administered Prices, 1968.

97. Hearings on Planning, Regulation, and Competition, 1968, p. 102.

98. Joe S. Bain, *Barriers to New Competition: Their Character and Consequence in Manufacturing Industries* (Cambridge: Harvard University Press, 1956), p. 245.

99. Hearings on Planning, Regulation, and Competition, 1968, p. 906.

100. "The Automobile Industry: A Case Study of Competition," p. 71.

101. Bain, *Barriers to New Competition,* p. 300.

102. Hearings on Planning, Regulation, and Competition, 1968, p. 907.

103. The "hold" of a brand or company name is particularly

binding in an oligopoly, where the names are fewer and more familiar.

104. Tim Metz, "GM to Change Signs of Dealers to Stress Name of Corporation," *Wall Street Journal,* June 12, 1968.

105. Hearings on Planning, Regulation, and Competition, 1968, pp. 104-105, 943.

106. In 1967 the motor vehicle and parts industry made purchases amounting to $14,428 million from its own sector, more than three times as much as the $4,074 million it spent on steel (Fortune Input-Output tally).

107. The sum of the "value added" by all sectors of the United States economy is equal to the Gross National Product. In 1967 this was about $739 billion. The sum of expenditures of all industries within their own sectors was about $116 billion. The ratio of value added to own-sector expenditures therefore averages 7-1 for American industry in general. For the auto industry, however, the 1967 figures were roughly $14.2 billion value added and $14.4 billion own-sector expenditures—a ratio of less than 1-1. Of 100 major industrial sectors, only three (sugar, copper, and thread) make smaller relative contributions to the GNP.

108. Hearings on Planning, Regulation, and Competition, 1968, p. 942.

109. *Congressional Record,* H6054, July 17, 1969.

110. Hearings on Planning, Regulation, and Competition, 1968, p. 352.

111. Frank C. Turner, Federal Highway Administrator, U.S. Department of Transportation, speech before 48th Annual Conference of the Western Association of State Highway Officials, June 3, 1969.

112. Hearings on Planning, Regulation, and Competition, 1968, p. 35.

113. Jack Anderson, "Washington Merry-Go-Round," *Washington Post,* November 11, 1969, p. B-11.

114. Colman McCarthy, "Three GMC School Buses and One Man's Ordeal," *Washington Post,* December 15, 1969; and "Troubled School Bus Operator Begins to 'Get Action'," *Washington Post,* December 1969.

115. Anderson, "Washington Merry-Go-Round."

116. It is perhaps indicative of the nature of these "competitive pressures" that smaller companies seem to do a much better job when it comes to innovations. Many of the features claimed as "first" by members of the Big Three were actually developed by independent inventors and companies whose names have been all but forgotten. A long list of such features is included in testimony by Dr. John Blair, Chief Economist, Subcommittee on Antitrust and Monopoly, U.S. Senate (Economic Concentration Hearings, 1965, Vol. 3).

117. Drew Pearson, "Washington Merry-Go-Round," *Washington Post,* February 16, 1968.

118. Hearings on Planning, Regulation, and Competition, 1968, p. 331.

119. Ronald A. Buel, "In Transit with the Road Lobbyists," *Wall Street Journal,* June 27, 1968.

120. Turner, June 3, 1969.

121. John A. Volpe, Secretary of Transportation, speech before the Annual Meeting of the Automobile Manufacturers' Association, June 20, 1969.

122. Pearson, "Washington Merry-Go-Round."

123. Franklin M. Fisher, Zvi Griliches, and Carl Kaysan, "The Costs of Automobile Model Changes Since 1949," *The Journal of Political Economy,* October 1962.

124. Hearings on Planning, Regulation, and Competition, 1968, p. 350.

125. Gordon D. Friedlander, "Technological Gap Traps Modern Man," *Washington Post,* August 10, 1969.

126. The Act was further weakened by the failure of Congress to include any criminal penalty for its violation even when such laws resulted in a loss of life.

127. "Autos 1968: Still Not Good Enough," *Consumer Reports,* April 1968.

128. "Jeep-Truck Safety Probed: Thousands of GIs Killed," *Washington Star,* 1969.

129. Anderson, November 17, 1969.

130. "Defects: The Art of Partial Assembly," *Consumer Reports,* May 1968.

131. Personal correspondence, January 1970.

132. Nicholas Von Hoffman, "When the Elite Buy 'Lemons'," *Washington Post,* January 9, 1970.

133. Hearings before the Subcommittee on Monopoly of the Select Committee on Small Business, U.S. Senate, 91st Cong., 1st session, on "The Role of Giant Corporations in the American and World Economies," Part I: Automobile Industry—1969, July 9, 10, and 11, 1969, p. 129.

134. Edward Daniels, Claim Manager, Detroit Automobile Interinsurance Exchange, speech before the American Society of Body Engineers, October 2, 1968. (cited in Hearings on Planning, Regulation, and Competition, 1968, p. 471).

135. Joseph Callahan, *Automotive News.*

136. "Auto bumper employs silicone liquid springs to absorb shock," *Product Engineering,* July 28, 1969, p. 91.

137. Daniels, October 2, 1968.

138. *NAII News,* National Association of Independent Insurers October 8, 1969.

139. In testimony before the House Committee on Interstate and Foreign Commerce in May, 1968, Walter Reuther described a situation reported by workers in one of the plants of a major auto manufacturer: ". . . if a ball joint retainer was missing or broken and squawked (reported) by the inspector, production supervision would instruct the repairman to 'punch the inspection ticket as if the defect had been repaired. . . . The report cited merely is one instance of what can, and often does, result from insistent demand that production lines keep moving no matter what the sacrifice in quality." And in the hearings on Planning, Regulation, and Competition, Ralph Nader testified that "last year in a Fisher Body plant in St. Louis a laborer by the name of Charles Gregory was objecting vociferously to a deficiency in the panel welding which he thought would permit the influx of carbon monoxide into the passenger compartment of some 1967 Chevrolets, and this gentleman was disciplined and told to mind his own business and shifted to another job and removed from his inspection duties."

140. Hearings before the Senate Antitrust and Monopoly

Subcommittee on "The Cost of Automobile Repair," October 1969.

141. Letter from James Roberts to Senator Hart.

142. Unresponsiveness of the auto magnates has been a prevailing pattern, judging by letters of complaint received by Hart. Another example: When Mrs. Boris Leavitt of Hanover, Pa., bought a new Cadillac Brougham, the power steering failed less than five miles from the dealership. Mrs. Leavitt wrote a registered letter to James Roche, but it was never acknowledged.

143. 1969 Yearbook, Automobile Manufacturers Association.

144. John W. Snow, "Government Training and Labor Shortage: A Study of the Labor Market for Automotive Mechanics" (unpublished PhD. dissertation, University of Virginia, 1965).

145. O'Brien, Hearings on Auto Pricing.

146. Philip H. Love, "Love On Life," *Washington Star,* October 27, 1969.

147. Norman C. Miller, "Car-Price Charade—In Making Up Tags, It Doesn't Pay to be Straight-Forward," *Wall Street Journal,* October 5, 1965.

148. "Autos: The Thinking Man's Car," *Time,* October 3, 1969, p. 93.

149. Letter from Thomas Mann, October 6, 1969.

150. Newsletter from Benjamin Rosenthal, undated.

151. Letter from Raymond Watts dated October 16, 1969.

152. Hearings on Auto Pricing.

153. *Automotive News,* October 13, 1969.

154. *Time* reported on August 30, 1968, that 512 Chrysler dealers were entirely leased or controlled by the Chrysler Corporation.

155. Hearings on "Role of Giant Corporations," p. 18.

156. Hammond, private interview, December 1969.

157. Bob Fendell, "Jersey Dealer Gains Writ Against Chrysler," *Automotive News,* March 31, 1969, p. 3.

158. By 1969, twenty states had enacted laws protecting dealers from unjustified terminations (or coercion by threats

of terminations) of franchises. One state (Hawaii) now requires manufacturers to be licensed and has provided for the suspension or revocation of the license of any manufacturer who sells a new car to a person in the state at a lower price than the price charged to a dealer.

159. "Suit Charges Chrysler Corporation with Conspiracy," *Automotive News,* March 31, 1969, p. 86.

160. Private interview.

161. Bob Fendell, "Mullane Campaigns for a 'Magna Carta' to Set Dealers Free," *Automotive News,* November 24, 1969, p. 1.

162. "Factory Competition Called No. 1 Problem," *Automotive News,* May 19, 1969, p. 3.

163. *Facts and Figures,* p. 10.

164. "Cases Charging General Motors Corporation with Violation of Section 5 of the Federal Trade Commission Act Involving Restraints of Trade," cited in hearings on Planning, Regulation, and Competition, 1968, p. 25.

165. *Ibid.,* p. 275.

166. "Auto Parts Monopoly," Technology Review, Vol. 71, No. 9 (Cambridge: Massachusetts Institute of Technology), July/Aug. 19, 1969, p. 81.

167. Hearings on Planning, Regulation, and Competition, 1968, p. 569.

168. *Ibid.,* p. 156.

169. GM claimed to have obtained the opposite results from a study of seven GM dealerships. The study was conducted by GM.

170. Robert M. Finlay, "Slack, Cole Eye Industry Woes, Auto Franchise," *Automotive News,* February 17, 1969, p. 1.

171. *Automotive News,* December 8, 1969, p. 1.

172. *Automotive News,* December 15, 1969, p. 12.

173. *Automotive News,* July 7, 1969, p. 10.

174. Hearings on Planning, Regulation, and Competition, 1968, pp. 44-71.

175. *Ibid.,* p. 933.

176. Hearings on "Role of Giant Corporations," pp. 407-466.

177. Hearings on Planning, Regulation, and Competition,

1968, p. 200.

178. *Ibid.,* pp. 428-446.

179. Less witty than Polonius, Mann had even more to say; his statement measured 41 pages in length.

180. *New York Times,* December 11, 1969, p. 1.

181. In an "open letter to Secretary Finch," *Automotive News* Engineering Editor Joseph Callahan wrote that with the exception of California, "The nation's forty-nine other states . . . certainly have their air pollution problems, but there is little or no evidence to link the automobile to these problems." *(Automotive News,* February 24, 1969, p. 2.)

182. Roche, speech at General Motors Safety Research and Development Laboratory dedication, Milford, Michigan, July 10, 1968.

183. Volpe, commencement address delivered at the U.S. Coast Guard Academy, New London, Connecticut, June 4, 1969.

184. Roche, speech at General Motors Housewarming, New York, October 3, 1968.

185. Joint hearings on "The Automobile Steam Engine," 1968.

186. Roche, October 3, 1968.

187. Joseph M. Callahan, "Speak Up for the Record, Knudson Tells Industry," *Automotive News,* January 20, 1969, p. 1.

188. Roche, "Understanding," p. 12.

189. Hearings on Planning, Regulation, and Competition, p. 17.

190. Peter Drucker, review of *My Years with General Motors,* in *Fortune,* July 1961.

191. i.e., new is always younger than old

192. " 'Automotive Riot' incited by Ad, Nader Charges," *Automotive News,* December 8, 1969, p. 4.

193. Staff Report from the Director, Bureau of Industry Guidance and Deceptive Practices, Federal Trade Commission, on Automobile Safety, Speed and Racing Advertising, November 15, 1966 (cited in Hearings on Planning, Regulation, and Competition, 1968, p. 456).

194. Clare E. Wise, "Design for Repairability," *Machine Design,* June 26, 1969, pp. 27-28.

195. Chilton Research Services and National Analysts, Inc.

196. Paul Ramirez, "Luxury Transit Service Fails to Lure Commuters from Autos in Flint," *Wall Street Journal,* Vol. CLXXIV, No. 45, 1969.

197. Norman Cousins, *Saturday Review,* 1967.

198. The hypocrisy of this gesture is amply demonstrated by the record of the recent two years, in which GM school buses went from bad to worse (as described in chapter 2).

199. *Facts and Figures,* p. 19.

200. Osborne T. Boyd, *The Washington Post,* January 7, 1970.

201. In *The Hidden Dimension,* Hall observes that intimate, personal, social, and public behavior produce varying needs for space—or distance—between an individual and the people with whom he is interacting. People would be uncomfortable, for example, standing as close to each other while waiting for a bus as they do while talking with friends at a party. Hall further notes that excessive crowding has been associated with severe psychological and physical disorders in animals—and speculates that crowding in cities may be equally dangerous to people, quite aside from the amount of space required for movement, etc.

202. Kent Cooper & Associates, Architects, Washington, D.C.

203. In a three-way race across Washington, D.C., in 1969, a bicycle easily defeated a bus and a car. ("Bicyclist Wins D.C. Commuter Race," *The Washington Star,* September 25, 1969, p. 1).

204. In Virginia and Maryland, the Skyline Drive and its northern counterparts have attracted large numbers of "vacation" homes, resulting in a proliferation of "No Trespassing" signs in the vicinity of the Trail. In some areas, hikers must now walk along the pavement. . . .

205. That pragmatic considerations can be quite irrelevant to the motivation of drivers is illustrated by a letter to the editor of *Automotive News* (December 8, 1969, p. 32), shortly

after the publication of an article criticizing the industry for putting so much research effort into such irrational features as the sound a car door makes when it closes (thunk!):

"In reply to all the unkind remarks flung at the auto industry about your "thunks." I want to thank you for spending countless man hours and money to make cars that stir my emotions.

"Though I don't talk about it, I really like hearing a rich sounding thunk! When I spend $$$$ for a car, I don't want a $.10 thunk. Though I am sometimes ashamed to admit it, deep down inside I enjoy your pampering of my emotions. An automobile is an extension of my ego and if you start playing to my reason, logic, etc . . . I'll stop buying your cars for other consumer goods that make me feel good.

"I know I don't need a cool looking car or even a new car every three years, but my emotions tell me different. Thank you for recognizing that I am human. Keep up the good work and I'll treat you well."

—The American People
Ferguson, Mo.

206. Eric Dahlquist, "The Hairiest Oldsmobile," *Motor Trend,* June, 1969, p. 30.

207. Hearings on Planning, Regulation, and Competition, 1968, pp. 455-456.

208. "How Safe Do We Choose to Be?" *Technology Review,* July/August, 1969, p. 72.

209. *Studies in Classic American Literature*

210. International Research and Technology *IDEAS,* September 1969, p. 96.

211. The usual economic model, even if it makes allowance for the indivisibilities of "public goods," tends to assume perfect information on the part of all participants.

212. *Automotive News,* September 1, 1969.

213. Arthur Selwyn Miller, "Business Morality: Some Unanswered (and Perhaps Unanswerable) Questions," *Annals of the American Academy of Political and Social Science,* January 1966 (cited in Hearings on Planning, Regulation, and Competition, 1968, p. 972).

214. William M. Blair, "DuBridge Says Public Is Ready to Pay Cost of Pollution Curbs," *The New York Times,* October 29, 1969.

215. White House Press Release, August 26, 1969.

216. Morton Mintz, "Business 'Social Costs' Debated," *Washington Post,* July 14, 1969, p. D-11.

217. *Congressional Record,* S2881, March 13, 1969.

218. Cited in "Getting to Work and Back," *Consumer Reports,* February 1965, p. 59.

219. Peter Millones, "Rates on Parking Target of Inquiry," *The New York Times,* August 21, 1969, p. 1.

220. News release, October 8, 1969.

221. John Hanrahan, "Insurance Dilemma: Do Firms Have Right to Say No?" *The Washington Post,* June 18, 1969, p. A-8; and "Car Insurance System Hardest on Young, Old, Military," June 19, 1969, p. A-25.

222. Gilbert B. Friedman, "Why Automobile Insurance Rates Keep Going Up," *Atlantic,* September 1969, p. 58.

223. Of course, some of this time would be spent in any case; even the most efficient system isn't instant. But *most* of the time spent on cars is wasted—and no one has discovered a way to get more.

224. Russell Baker, "Observer: Shoulder to the Boulder, Dream Boaters!" *The New York Times,* August 28, 1969.

225. "Economy," *Walden.*